The Nitpicker's Guide to the Movies

the Movies

Volume 3

By

Will Nuessle

The Nitpicker's Guide to the Movies
Volume 3

You should take the above seriously, as he is a ninja.

Table of Contents

Foreword

The middle of the road! Volume Three!

And an explanation is perhaps due. If you've looked at the contents list for this book, and gauged it against what you found on Wikipedia as the "Top 50 Grossing Movies of All Time,"[1] you will have noticed some discrepancies. You didn't see Terminator II on that list, nor Empire Strikes Back or Raiders of the Lost Ark.

What gives?

Lemme explain. First, this being a Top Grossing nitpicker gets a little frustrating. The Top 50 list has drastically changed in the two years since I started this experiment. Ten of the top fifty films as of today, January 15, 2011, weren't even in theaters when I started--which means that if I was that concerned about being completely accurate, I'd have to throw out 20,000+ words of writing (one entire volume in this series!) to get up-to-date. And as much as I love you all, I have a life outside of my nitpicking.

The other problem: well...the reason I chose the Top 50 Grossing Movies to nitpick was twofold: to find movies that everybody could relate to, and to find what should be really great movies. It seemed to make sense at the time: the ones that have made the most money must be the best, right?

Yeah, I don't know what I was thinking either. It's been a long, hard road--for every Star Wars IV, there's been a Star Wars III. For every Fellowship of the Ring, there's been, like, twenty-seven Harry Potter movies. And my spirit started to be broken, and I began to doubt my place in this world...

---

[1] Probably need to make it Top 100 by now (2017)

...and then I realized that the Force was not with me when I saw <u>Indiana Jones and the Kingdom of the Crystal Skull</u> on the top 50 list. What is with the moviegoing public? We couldn't collectively realize how truly awful that movie was? I can't speak for you, but I refused to see that movie again, even to pick it apart. It wasn't worth the cost of living in an insane asylum the rest of my life. So I made an executive decision--it's my book, after all--and nitpicked <u>Raiders of the Lost Ark</u> instead. An order of magnitude better, it also deserves to be in the Top 50 much more than Indy 4 ever will. The same goes for <u>Terminator II</u>, chosen to replace <u>Transformers 2</u> (you tell me, which is a better film? I thought so).

In the case of <u>Empire Strikes Back</u>, I nitpicked that instead of <u>Inception</u> for three reasons: when I needed to write the review, <u>Inception</u> still wasn't available on DVD, I wasn't huge on nitpicking that movie anyway (it's all a dream, how do you nitpick a dream?) and finally every other one of the six <u>Star Wars</u> movies is on the Top 50 list (for now), and if I had to go through the horror of watching that dreadful prequel again, I was also going to balance the experience with <u>all</u> of the classic Wars movies.

So now you know. Hope there's no terrible disappointment.

If this is your first NGM experience, welcome aboard--and keep your eyes open for volumes 1-2, coming soon! (Accident with a hard drive and a time machine--no time to go into explanation here.)

Enough with the foreword...<u>forward</u>!

#21:   Lord of the Rings: The Fellowship of the Ring

Ruminations: Peter Jackson's not perfect (King Kong ran about forty-five minutes longer than it needed to) but for my money, he and his crew did up the Lord of the Rings trilogy very well. No, not everything matches the books (and believe me, I'll mention the moments where it should have,) but the characters, the setting, the adventure leaps off the screen. The three movies are incredibly beautiful thrill-rides, like I had hoped for.

For the record, though, the books are even better.

Note: settle in, grab some coffee. Like the other two movies (found in Volume 1 and 2 of this book series, this review covers the extended, elongated, full-bore film-nerd version of the movie. I have a lot of nits to cover...

0:00:52-Let's just jump right in with a grungy nit. In the opening monologue, Cate Blanchett talks about the history of the ring, concluding with "For none now live who remember it." Well, obviously somebody remembers it, because someone has to tell us what happened...

0:02:08-Nobody ever explains why the ring doesn't make Sauron invisible.

0:02:10-Sauron's spiky finger-sheaths appear to be riveted to his glove. So how did he get the Ring on? It's much too small to fit over those protrusions.

0:02:47-In the epic opening battle, how come Elrond isn't helmeted?

0:02:52-He could use a helmet, because the archers behind those sword-carrying Elves fire right through the line (we see an arrow muss Elrond's hair). Does that make any sense? Are the elves just showing off? It would seem like having the front line <u>kneel</u> so the archers could fire <u>over</u> them would be a lot wiser.

0:02:57-Apparently there are cowards in Orc land, too--in the opening arrow barrage, some of the Orcs fall over without taking a hit. Then again, the Elf swords might be magical. Watch the guy on the end, the sword doesn't even touch him, yet he falls!

0:03:04-Right before the voiceover says "Victory was near", one of the elves stabs downward with his sword, accompanied by a sharp metallic sound. Don't they teach in sword-fighting school <u>not</u> to try and pierce metal plate? (Go for the chinks, man!)

0:03:55-Sauron's fingers (including the Ring) get cut off...and he <u>explodes</u>. That's never explained, either. (Talk about your Achilles heel. Should've kept that hand in his pocket!)

0:04:46-"but the Ring of power has a will of its own." Nobody--even Tolkien--ever explains how an inanimate object managed to get a will of its own. At least it was something romantic like a ring, eh? ("The Teapot of Slagathor has a will of its own...")

0:05:03-Isildur's disappearing act is obviously blue-screen. And is he standing in a hole? He appears to be only three feet off the ground.

0:05:36-"History became legend. <u>Legend became myth</u>." That's very poetic, but according to my dictionary, completely redundant.

0:06:10-We get a glimpse (still in the prologue here, people) around Gollum's cave. According to Tolkien, fish were all that the creature had to eat, so you'd think he would eat every last one. But we see at least one whole fish on the ground. Also: if he's "deep in the Misty Mountains," where is the light shining on him coming from? The Misty Mountains Cavern Tour?

0:09:11-As we (finally) get a look at Hobbiton, one of the precious Hobbits drops a load of firewood--right in front of the door. Why would he do that? "The pile's over there, you half-sized half-wit!"

0:10:12-Note: according to Bilbo, "It is no bad thing to celebrate a simple life." Call me a hobbit if you must, but I am right there with him.

0:15:45-The light reflecting onto Gandalf's face as he stands at Bilbo's front door is not happening naturally. Some poor Production Assistant is crouched by the door with a silver reflector, bouncing the daylight back at him. (You can trust me, I have a film degree.)

0:27:50-Gandalf, to Bilbo: "I'm not trying to rob you!" As he says this, his head/hair change as the shot changes. More changes (0:28:11) during "All your long years, we've been friends." He's right next to Bilbo, then a foot away, then right next to him again.

0:29:05-Note: this movie does a lot of things right--and one of those is how when Bilbo drops the Ring, it doesn't bounce. It just lands and stays, as if the Ring carried the weight of the world...marvelous!

0:29:25-Gandalf: "I'm sure you will, my dear friend." Is he practicing his ventriloquism? His lips don't seem to be moving.

0:29:45-Seems like a bad idea for one-hundred-and-eleven-year-old Bilbo to be toddling off alone in the middle of the night.

0:36:36-Gandalf tells Frodo to keep the Ring secret and safe, then rides away. Some time later, as things are starting to get creepy around the Shire, he suddenly returns. It would be nice if he had said something, light a lamp, maybe, to let Frodo know that he was back, rather than lunging out of the darkness at him.

0:37:49-Interesting that the Ring's legend is written in the language of Mordor (which I shall not utter here) yet when translated to English, the poem still rhymes.

0:38:12-The sound-effect guy had so much work to do he slept through one bit: as Frodo and Gandalf talk about what must be done with the Ring, Frodo sets the teapot down, picks up his cup and sits down all without accompanying noise.

0:40:11-A big deal is made about how Gollum, under torture, reveals two words: "Shire" and "Baggins." In The Hobbit, Bilbo does indeed tell Gollum his name, but he never says a word about the Shire, so how would Gollum know?

0:44:16-As Sam balks at the journey ahead and Frodo talks him into it, Frodo changes position several times as the shot changes.

0:47:28-As Saruman and Gandalf walk in the sunshine, the position of their staffs gets wonky with the changing shots. One moment is as Gandalf says "Under my very nose."

0:49:27-Maybe Gandalf is getting old. Saruman starts trapping him in the room by magically closing the doors. Four separate times Gandalf goes for a set of doors only to have it close in front of him. Seems like after the second time he would get the idea. Also, Saruman has power enough to snatch Gandalf's staff out of his hand, and Gandalf can't get it back? Poor guy.

0:50:20-Gandalf changes position as the shot changes when Saruman throws him against the wall.

0:51:01-Saruman must have power to burn. He makes Gandalf revolve by the neck on the floor (I can't imagine what the stuntman had to go through for that shot) and then sends him upwards, now revolving at the waist. Saruman also spares some power to flip Gandalf over so he can see the roof of the tower coming.

0:51:15-<u>The Will Award</u>: lucky for all of us, and for the rest of the story, that Saruman toys with Gandalf and imprisons him, instead of killing him when he had the chance.

0:52:33-As the four hobbits start to fall over the cliff, Sam and Frodo change position as the shot changes.

0:53:45-The hobbits get off the road, and a few seconds later a Rider appears. There's no sound to announce his coming. We looked down the road from Frodo's point of view; if that Rider had galloped in, he should've made more noise--if he was walking his horse it should've taken longer. Either way, there should be some leaf-crunching sounds.

0:54:02-The first Rider we see...are those <u>nails</u> sticking out of the horse's foot? What is the point of those?

0:54:44-Merry throws something and the Rider turns away. He didn't see Merry throwing the object? He's <u>right there</u>.

0:56:00-During the Rider chase, one of said Riders is silhouetted by a bright light on the horizon...and that light is what, exactly? And how fast can those Hobbits run that a full-grown horse-and-rider can't catch them?

0:57:01-Are the Riders cat-like, afraid of water? It's of the <u>utmost importance</u> that the Rider get the ring, yet he doesn't even try to follow the Hobbits into the river. Picked a horse that couldn't swim, I suppose.

0:57:16-Whoops--Pippin says the nearest crossing is 20 miles away. Didn't know they used the term <u>miles</u> in Middle Earth.

0:57:40-When the hobbits reach Bree, the gatekeeper opens a human-high little door to look out of the gate, then does the same lower down with a Hobbit-high door. Is this second door really necessary? Can't the gatekeeper just look down a little? (Moreover, after looking through the gate, the keeper still seems to be surprised to find Hobbits outside.)

0:58:08-As Frodo and Sam step through the gate at Bree, their position changes as the shot changes. (Sam steps through the door twice.)

0:58:11-Merry and Pippin are still in the line of the door when the shot changes and it swings shut without hitting them.

1:00:08-"It comes in pints?" Merry seems envious of Pippin's new information, yet both Pippin's new mug and the one Merry already has look exactly the same.

1:01:26-Pippin isn't especially quick on the uptake either--did he not hear Frodo refer to himself as Underhill?

1:03:11-Sam, Merry and Pippin burst in on Frodo and Aragorn, ready to defend Frodo to the death. Pippin's kind of late to the party--looking out of the room, only his shadow is visible on the wall when suddenly the shot changes, and he's halfway into the room.

1:03:31-The Riders blow through the gate and knock the gatekeeper down, and the gate falls flat to the ground. Must be very muddy for the gatekeeper to disappear into the ground like that.

1:05:38-As Aragorn says "Into the wild," and heroically walks past the camera, the shot wobbles--almost, perhaps, as if the hero's bow heroically smacks right into the camera.

1:05:48-"How do we know this Strider is a friend?" The hobbits change positions during that line.

1:05:53-Sam, about Aragorn: "A servant of the enemy would look fairer and feel fouler, if you get my meaning." 100 points to the first person who can name <u>any</u>

servant of the enemy who looks fair. (Hmm. Gollum, the Riders, the orcs, the cave-troll, the Balrog, Wormtongue, Saruman...)

1:06:00-As the hobbits question if Strider is good or bad, Frodo changes positions throughout the scene.

1:06:18-With so many birds as Sauron's spies, does it make sense for Aragorn and the Hobbits to walk through clearings?

1:07:36-To feed his hungry Hobbits, Aragorn comes into scene carrying a deer. It's not safe to light a fire, and there's no evidence of one in the later shot. I'm sorry I missed that meal, I just <u>love</u> raw deer!

1:09:03-The Ring is (as previously mentioned) inscribed with the language of Mordor, which I still will not utter here. Since Sauron would presumably speak mainly the language of Mordor, it's nice that he talks to Saruman and Frodo in English.

1:09:14-"What orders from Mordor?" Besides being a poet, the orc that says this changes position between shots.

1:10:56-Note: in the movie, Aragorn just hands out four swords. (Makes one wonder where he got them from, huh?) The tale in Tolkien's book of how the hobbits <u>really</u> got their swords is much more interesting, and worth a read.

1:10:59-Why does Aragorn wait as long as he does to arm the hobbits?

1:12:20-Right before we see the Nazgul on the hilltop, the hobbits change position as the shot changes. The Nazgul do too: as the five advance on the hobbits, the second from the right is a step ahead of the others--shot changes and suddenly all five are in a nice semi-circle. Also there's a shadow on the ground that doesn't seem to correspond to anything we've seen on the hilltop.

1:12:33-You know, I don't think the Nazgul are really all <u>that</u> bad. They're just focused, is all. I mean, on Weathertop they advance on Frodo and push Sam, Merry and Pippin out of the way. They <u>push them out of the way</u>. How hard would it be to just stab them and be done with it? (The Head of the Nazgul's gonna regret that one later, I betcha...)

1:12:40-After the Nazgul knocks Frodo to the ground, he changes position when the shot changes.

1:12:55-It's pretty amazing that five Ringwraiths couldn't get the Ring away from one Hobbit. Yes, Aragorn arrived to save the day, but still...I wouldn't want to be the one who has to call Sauron and tell him.

1:13:46-When Frodo put the ring on in the bar, everybody around became indistinct shadows. On Weathertop, all the Nazgul appear as they used to be, the human kings. This is all correct. The Nazgul have gone over to the shadows, and only the power of the Ring can show their true forms. However, when Aragorn jumps into things, he's recognizable. Does he get special Ring treatment for being a hero?

1:14:31-It's a nice move, in my opinion, when Aragorn throws his torch right into the last Nazgul's face. However, when he does so, the haft of the torch is left sticking maybe eight inches out of the Rider's hood--until the shot changes, when suddenly about two feet of torch is sticking out. (Did the Nazgul tell a lie, perhaps?)

1:16:00-Rather fortunate for Gandalf, trapped on the pinnacle of Orthanc, that a moth happened by, that he could converse with said moth (Radagast was the one that had a way with birds, after all) and that the moth could go and talk to the eagle...

1:16:30-As the orcs fell the trees around Saruman's hacienda, the tree they throw into the pit is on its side, but when the shot changes it's suddenly pointing downwards.

1:17:05-I don't even want to <u>know</u> what an orc-making recipe calls for. (Betcha it's not cinnamon.) Anyway, who told the orc to arise from his mud-cradle in a slow, dramatic fashion, rather than horking and retching and throwing mud everywhere?

1:18:32-Arwen surprises Aragorn with the edge of her blade. This seems a dumb thing to do to a hardened warrior-type. She's lucky she didn't get her arm cut off.

1:18:45-Arwen the beautiful shows up (Liv Tyler can come to my rescue <u>anytime</u>) and tells Frodo, in Elvish, that she is there to help. She knows English--does Frodo know elvish? Wouldn't it be more comforting for him to hear that she's there to help him in a language he understands? (I mean, she could talk to <u>me</u> in Ancient Greek and I would be comforted, but still...)

1:22:55-Lucky that Arwen's magical tidal wave knows not to sweep her away too, since she's standing <u>right there</u>.

1:24:41-Frodo, safe in Rivendell, changes position in his bed as the shot changes. He's above the pillow, below the pillow, above the pillow...

1:27:04-This is pretty grungy, but it's a fairly obvious blue-screen effect as Frodo reunites with his comrades. Nice touch that Merry's chewing something, though.

1:27:39-If you're a fan of the books, freeze the DVD and take a closer look at the book Bilbo shows Frodo. There are some nice references to <u>The Hobbit</u> in the graphics. Kudos!

1:29:00-Sam changes positions as he says "We did what Gandalf wanted, didn't we?"

1:33:09-This one's for you, Ma: Aragorn really shouldn't try to read by moonlight--that's superbad for your eyes.

1:34:39-I'm so happy: Boromir, fiddling around with things that don't concern him, cuts his hand on Isildur's broken sword. He cuts his <u>left</u> hand, but as he strides haughtily away he puts his <u>right</u> hand to his mouth.

1:34:55-What are the chances that <u>3,000</u> years after Isildur's passing, Aragorn is his <u>only</u> heir?

1:36:43-Arwen and Aragorn are having a moment, and she gives him her priceless necklace. She's wearing the necklace in one shot, then puts it in his hand in the next. There's time enough for her to get it off, but she never raises her arms. Did she take it off magically?

1:41:11-Gimli foolishly destroys an axe trying to bust up the Ring. (More on that later.) Elrond then says, "The Ring cannot be destroyed, Gimli." Would have been nice for somebody to mention that <u>before</u> Gimli busted a perfectly good axe and showered everybody with sharp metal fragments...

1:42:24-Boromir, on Mordor: "The very air you breathe is a poisonous fume." Is he waxing poetic? Talking about a place he's never been? Maybe he's just full of it--whatever the reason, his statement can't be accurate, because all sorts of good folks breathe Mordor's air in the later films, and nobody seems to suffer for it.

1:42:56-During the Council on what to do with the Ring, that same Ring's reflections are inconsistent throughout the scene.

1:43:28-As Frodo repeats "I will take it," and Gandalf hears him, big G changes positions between the wide and close-up shot.

1:43:40-In Tolkien's book, there is a prophesy about a halfling "standing forth" when the time came, so when Frodo says he'll take the Ring to Mordor it makes sense. They don't put that in the film, so you have a big squabble--"Don't let the elf have it," "We should use it," and so forth...then Frodo says he'll take it and everybody agrees that's a great idea for no apparent reason.

1:44:21-Gimli dwarfishly smashes an axe on the Ring in an attempt to destroy it. Then minutes later he stands with the Company, axe in hand. Apparently, he grabbed the axe of the dwarf next to him, used <u>that</u> axe and not his own to try and destroy the Ring. Knowing how proud a race the dwarves are, I would think that if Gimli expected his axe-blow to do the job, he would use no other weapon than his own. (Still, that's the official Peter Jackson explanation as to how Gimli destroys one axe and immediately has another to offer in service to Frodo.) On to Disk Two...

0:05:51-As the Company's road turns sour, Gimli encourages them to go through the Mines of Moria. Gandalf: "No, Gimli--I will not take the road through Moria unless I have no other choice." He says nothing further. If he <u>knows</u> something about what's going on down there, it would be <u>nice</u> of him to share with Gimli. The dwarf has family in the Mines, after all.

0:06:04-Is Pippin a big sissy? As Boromir teaches Merry and Pip something about sword fighting, Pippin jumps back, shaking his hand after Boromir's sword hits his. Except Boromir's sword didn't come anywhere <u>near</u> his hand.

0:06:11-As the Company rests and Boromir teaches Merry and Pippin, the positions of all three are out-of-sync between certain shots. (When the Hobbits tackle Boromir, and when the three fall down, among others)

0:06:20-The Company hides as an entire murder of crows wings past. Does it make sense to send the whole flock out together? You could cover a <u>lot</u> more ground sending them out in ones and twos, and they wouldn't be so darned <u>obvious</u> to boot.

0:07:18-Whoa! Where'd that enormous mountain come from? I've looked carefully through the shots of the company on that hilltop, and though there are wide, sweeping, cover-the-whole-horizon shots, I don't see the huge, brooding Mount Caradhras until suddenly Gandalf sees fit to mention it. Then poof! We look up and there it is.

0:07:38-When Frodo falls on the snow and the Ring slips out into the open, we get a good look at his neck/upper chest...why isn't Frodo wearing the Mithril coat Bilbo gave him? And when does he decide to put it on? He's sure wearing it when the cave troll spears him.

0:08:35-Production crews hate mirror-sunglasses, and I'll bet the crew wasn't too fond of the big, round, polished knob in the middle of Boromir's shield, either. Right after he gives the Ring back to Frodo he turns, and we get a nice view of the whole production team reflected in that knob.

0:09:41-Sure lucky nobody was hurt on Caradhras when the side of the <u>mountain</u> caved in!

0:11:58-Gandalf makes Frodo decide what path to take, and seems upset at his choice, without giving him <u>any</u> information about what waits in Moria. That's not very nice of him.

0:13:08-Approaching Moria, Frodo and Gandalf have a bit of a chat about the ring. Not only does Gandalf change positions between at least one shot in this scene, but after they talk, Gimli points out the doors of Moria...and the rock face, indeed the whole hillside the Company has been standing against is suddenly gone.

0:14:10-It looks <u>very</u> cool, but is it convenient that the Mines of Moria (a business venture, after all) can only open their doors at night? "UPS, please arrive after dark, and dude, mind the monster in the pool out front."

0:14:36-Does it make any sense at all for Gandalf to <u>push</u> the magically sealed doors of Moria?

0:15:58-I've been holding my tongue on all of the ways the filmmakers have changed something from Tolkien's original book, but in <u>The Fellowship of the Ring</u> it's Gandalf who figures out the riddle to Moria, not Frodo. (They make the big G look stupid, and I can't abide that.)

0:17:17-Does the creature in the lake want the Ring? It picks up Frodo and only Frodo out of the whole Company. When we meet Shelob the monstrous spider later, she doesn't care about Rings...why does this fellow?

0:17:35-Nice of the creature to dangle Frodo around for awhile, give the others a chance to fight back, instead of pulling him straight under and disappearing.

0:19:01-"Let us hope our presence here goes unnoticed." Is he kidding? With the racket they all made getting in, and the bright, magical light Gandalf is throwing around?

0:19:56-For someone who hopes his presence in the Mines will go unnoticed, Gandalf sure gives a loud, unnecessary history lesson.

0:20:22-That light of Gandalf's really is magic: he moves his staff up and down as he walks, yet the shadows don't move. (Almost as if the light source was something else!)

0:21:00-Gandalf changes position as he first faces the three doorways.

0:21:40-Gandalf's hair changes position as he talks about Gollum. Also, several shots of Frodo show Gandalf's beard still moving, as if he was talking, though there's no dialogue. (0:23:46, for example)

0:21:41-Frodo realizes they're being followed, and Gandalf, who knew this (that man just refuses to share information) says Gollum has been following them since Rivendell. So...old skin-and-bones made it up Caradhras? Where was he?

0:22:26-Is Gollum somehow different from the other evil characters in this story? Gandalf rips Frodo a new one for suggesting Bilbo should have offed the creature--yet hundreds of orcs and goblins and cave trolls and evil men and Ringwraiths are killed without anybody mourning. What's different about ol' Smeagol? (Besides the fact that he's needed for the story's climax?)

0:23:56-When Gandalf realizes which door to take, and says "It's that way," the shot cuts to Aragorn, Boromir and Gimli, who have a warm light on them that doesn't make sense.

0:24:30-This is an underground mine. This whole thing, likely, had to be dug out by hand. What is the purpose, then, of Dwarrowdelf, which looks like nothing more than a gigantic room? There are no forges, carts, tools, anything...was this the dwarves' dance hall?

0:26:00-Gandalf, in Balin's tomb, picks up an enormously thick book, which falls open to exactly the page he wants.

0:26:31-Dwarvish is indeed a flowery language. Gandalf reads a page with eleven lines of dwarf writing: "We cannot get out. The shadow moves in the dark. We cannot get out. They are coming." It took eleven full lines of Dwarvish to say that?

0:27:45-So all of the talking and walking about and slamming of the front door and Gandalf's bobbing magical light doesn't arouse the orcs...but one (admittedly loud) dead guy falling into a well brings the whole place down on the Company? They don't just send out one orc to see if something's up? What if it's a false alarm?

0:28:03-Sam looks at Frodo's sword. Frodo <u>pulls his sword out</u> and by Golly it's shining blue. How did Sam know this, since the sword was <u>sheathed</u>?

0:28:15-I guess I wouldn't make a good action hero. The orcs (who are fortunately bad archers) lob two arrows into the door <u>right</u> by Boromir's head as he looks out, and he stands there for two whole seconds looking perturbed. If somebody came <u>this close</u> to hitting me with an arrow, I would've scrambled back as fast as possible, even if I landed on my butt doing so.

0:29:30-It is truly remarkable, almost miraculous, that a whole company of orcs and a giant cave troll squeeze into this little space for furious battle, and yet none of our heroes are seriously threatened <u>except</u> Frodo, who just happens to be extra protected.

0:29:45-Legolas gets the opportunity to draw down on the cave troll, and he shoots the beast in the <u>shoulder</u>. Go for the <u>eyes</u>, you pointy-eared moron!

0:30:05-Boromir is thrown fifteen feet into a stone wall, yet breaks no bones. Remarkable. Then after Aragorn takes time out to save Boromir's life, the two have a quick "Hey, just saved your life" moment. (0:30:18) Guys, there's a CAVE TROLL in here!

0:30:53-The troll swings his chain around a pillar, Legolas stops it with his <u>foot</u>, then there's enough tension and the chain stays in place so he can run up it to the troll's head. Riiiiight.

0:32:06-Now Aragorn is thrown ten feet into a stone pillar, yet remains unharmed. Incredible.

0:32:55-The Mithril coat Frodo is wearing keeps the cave troll's spear from piercing him. So why does the spear keep sticking out of him? It's like seven feet long--that's a heavy pole, which if it turned on the mail coat, isn't supported by anything.

0:33:57-Frodo says, and I quote: "I'm not hurt." So...why did he gasp, and wheeze, and collapse to the floor for thirty seconds? Dramatic effect?

0:35:00-Why are orcs able to crawl on the ceiling? Down stone pillars?

0:35:18-I'm going to geek out just a tiny bit: Bilbo's sword, which Frodo carries into Moria, glows because the elves made it that way. Sting is one of three blades found in the goblin cave in <u>The Hobbit</u>--one of the others, Gandalf's sword Glamdring, <u>also</u> glows blue when orcs are about, which means it <u>should</u> be glowing throughout the Moria battle scenes. But it doesn't. (Fifteen hundred points to the first person who can tell me the third sword's name and where it ended up...)

0:35:27-Despite the fact that the Balrog supposedly kills Gandalf, it's really lucky that the thing came along. There are <u>hundreds</u>, maybe <u>thousands</u> of orcs surrounding our heroes. They're <u>dead</u>. Then the Balrog steps in and the orcs run away.

0:37:11-The Mines of Moria is a business, supposedly...yet these steps have no railing whatsoever, standing <u>hundreds</u> of feet in the air. Even before they started crumbling, these things were a safety hazard...obviously Middle-Earth has no OSHA. Also, everybody turns a corner on these incredibly dangerous stairs and Boromir leaps down from the flight above--which could easily have resulted in someone being knocked off to their death. Stupid thing to do!

0:38:43-Sure is lucky the orcs are terrible archers, and that only three or four of the <u>thousands</u> we saw a moment ago remain available to shoot at our heroes--because they are on that ridiculous collapsing stair for some time. Also lucky that ridiculous stair fell forward instead of sideways while Aragorn and Frodo were still on it, huh?

0:40:08-I think OSHA would have a thing or two to say about the bridge of Khazad-Dum, too. It's the <u>only</u> way out of the Mines on this side of the mountains, yet it has no railings and is only wide enough for one person. The Dwarves may be clever masons, but they sure suck at infrastructure...

0:40:20-For that matter, why does Gandalf even bother facing the Balrog? It's not like that thing is going to get across the tiny bridge...

0:40:45-As Gandalf fights the Balrog, the light from his staff becomes blue, yet the light on his face is still white.

0:44:46-As Frodo enters the wood of Lothlorien, Galadriel speaks into his mind, telling him he brings great evil with him. The poor hobbit is only on this quest because he has to be, and now some bitchy elf-queen he doesn't even know is telling him all this by invading his mind? Give the poor guy a break!

0:45:14-Peripheral Vision Problem: Gimli is talking smack about the elves when suddenly they're surrounded by elven archers. All of them look surprised--did the elves beam in, or something?

0:48:00-Lothlorien seems to be nothing but stairs upon stairs upon stairs...these elves must have <u>terrific</u> calves. (At least these stairs have railings.)

0:48:20-I was just commending the elves on having railings on their stairs, and then we get to Galadriel's chamber, which has a flat, smooth floor and no railing whatsoever against a hundred-foot fall.

0:48:58-When Celeborn and Galadriel reach the bottom of the short stair, the shot changes and suddenly Galadriel's eyes are closed.

0:51:28-Galadriel sure has a funny way of making people relax. She tells the Company to rest, and not be afraid...and then she speaks into Frodo's mind and does that scary eye thing. I really don't think I would have an easy time <u>resting</u> after that whammy.

0:56:58-It's tricky to nitpick magic, but it sure is accommodating of Galadriel's magic mirror to come complete with <u>sound-effects</u>.

0:58:09-While at the mirror, Galadriel speaks into Frodo's head again, and this time Frodo telepathically speaks back. Funny, I didn't know Frodo could <u>do</u> that... (And I wonder how Frodo knew he could!)

1:18:27-As Aragorn and Frodo have a moment on the hilltop, it's Aragorn, this time, who realizes orcs are near because Sting is glowing. Yet once again, <u>Sting is sheathed at the time</u>.

1:18:46-Why exactly is the <u>leader</u> of the Uruk-hai the only one without a helmet?

1:18:52-Nice of the orcs that attack Aragorn to follow the movie-rule "Thou Shalt Attack One At A Time." It's one against, like, forty: if they had rushed him, he'd probably have been killed.

1:19:05-Aragorn fights off the orc company on the hilltop--as he climbs the short stone steps, there are continuity errors to be found.

1:20:01-Frodo is heading down to the boats, trying to leave on his quest. Merry and Pippin see him, wave him over to where they're hiding. All Frodo does is shake his head no, and somehow Merry divines that Frodo is leaving. Is Galadriel's telepathic power still in effect?

1:21:05-You just can't get good help these days. We all heard Saruman order the half-lings captured "alive and unspoiled", yet until Boromir steps in, there's an orc bearing down on Merry and Pippin with an axe.

1:22:47-Too bad Aragorn's attack rule didn't apply to Boromir. He was doing okay until Big Bad Orc stepped in with his <u>arrows</u>, a clear violation of the rules...

1:24:17-As Merry and Pippin charge the orcs, after Boromir falls, they change position as the shot changes.

1:25:04-The Big Bad Orc takes a hit from Aragorn. Baddie hasn't even stopped rolling when the shot changes and he's on his feet, sword and shield in hand. Then as he raises his arm, the shot changes and he raises his arm again.

1:25:11-There's no tree behind Aragorn as he and Big Bad start fighting, but the orcs must put one in <u>really</u> quickly so that Big Bad can pin Aragorn to it with his shield. (Maybe it's an Ent.) Also, if that shield is really tight to his neck, he shouldn't be able to get his head out from behind it as he does a moment later.

1:25:15-As Aragorn and Big Bad tussle, their position changes as the shot changes (a lot).

1:25:34-Nice of the Big Bad Orc to take a moment, during his fight with Aragorn, to lick his own blood (eww) off the knife--giving Aragorn a chance to grab his sword and knock away the thrown knife a moment later. (Which reportedly Viggo Mortensen really did, on the first take, no less!)

1:25:45-Aragorn stabs Big Bad, and the orc pulls himself forward on Aragorn's blade to roar at him. Then Aragorn yanks his sword out of Big Bad's body and beheads him. I've done a little sword training myself, and I don't think he would be able to clear the blade from Big Bad's body without stepping further away.

1:26:00-Once Aragorn dispatches Big Bad, he runs back to Boromir's side, dodging a bunch of corpses that weren't around during the fight and have magically appeared. Even more fun: as Aragorn bounds down the hill, one of the dead orcs lifts his head to watch. Apparently even orcs know how to play possum!

1:27:34-Boromir, to Aragorn: "I would have followed you, my brother." A: suuuure he would have, and 2: is he just being figurative to call Aragorn his brother? His brother is Faramir--and since Aragorn is the heir that will depose Boromir's father, Denethor, from his stewardship, it seems like a strange thing for Boromir to say. (But he is dying, after all.)

1:30:02-Earlier, when the Company was boating down the river, the boats were the right size for Aragorn and Boromir, and big for the hobbits. Now when Frodo and Sam take a boat, the boat seems the right size for them. It can't be both.

1:32:10-Aragorn wouldn't dare go to the eastern shore until nightfall, for fear of patrolling orcs, yet Frodo and Sam reach the eastern shore and apparently have no orc problems at all. Boy, Aragorn's really not having a good day...

1:32:15-Considering that when a person dies, all the blood collects in the lower portion of their body, Boromir sure should look a lot paler in his death-boat.

1:33:00-Gimli laments that the Ring has gone on without him. "Then it has all been in vain. The Fellowship has failed." Aragorn: "Not if we hold true to each other." Suddenly the music is hopeful, Gimli and Legolas's faces brighten, and they take after the orcs. Huh? The whole point of the Fellowship was to protect the Ring, and that has indeed failed. I have to go with Gimli on this one. Whether they find Merry and Pippin or not, if the Ring falls into Sauron's hand its all over for everybody. (Then again, we have established that Aragorn is not having his best day ever)

      1:33:33-Aragorn tells the others that they must travel light to hunt orc. Okay, but y'all might consider taking just a pinch of <u>food</u> with you...

#22:   Star Wars III: Revenge of the Sith

Ruminations: I feel like I phoned this one in. Because I didn't want to watch this movie again. I think even more than I didn't want to watch Titanic again.

The classic movies are such fun, and such wonderful bits of my childhood, that to watch the prequel, especially III, just hurts deep inside.

Interesting note: there are more than two thousand visual effects shots in this movie...and yet this is the only one of all six Star Wars movies not to be nominated for a Visual Effects Academy Award.

This movie is also the only PG-13 rated out of all the Star Wars movies...and I personally feel a lot of what is seen on screen violates that rating. Lucas—not that you care what I think, but I ain't happy!

If you haven't read any of the other Nitpicking Volumes (why not? They're fun too...) you won't know that I have a specifically Star Wars nitpicking book, written by T.A. Chapin and Polly Luttrell. One that covers five of the six Star Wars movies--and yet doesn't catch everything, which made watching the movies extra fun this time around. Kind of a competition to find things they missed.

But I don't even have that with this movie, since the version I have of their book was out before III...so I have nothing to check!

Sigh...

-0:03:00 Why do our two heroes go through the space battle on their way to Grievous' ship? They could more easily and safely fly around all of this, couldn't they?

-0:03:10 Once per Star Wars review—<u>boy</u>, space is <u>loud</u>, ain't it?

-0:04:51 Whiny Anakin's in trouble. Maybe if I didn't hate him so much, I would care about that

-0:05:32 I'm not sure how the buzz droids hold on to the ships

-0:05:44 This buzz droid is disabling Kenobi's ship. Why doesn't Kenobi use the Force to get the bugger off?

-0:06:37 Ah, so that Anakin can get the droid off using a high-speed starfighter collision. Which makes so much more sense than using the Force

-0:07:19 Why are shield generators always <u>outside</u> the shield they generate?

-0:08:19 Watching all the frantic, blink-and-you-miss-it action (the stuff that takes the place of a good story), I figure today's generation must just sleep right through the classic Star Wars movies

-0:08:34 Why is the <u>robot</u> coughing?

-0:09:25 "Did you press the Stop button?" "No, did you?" <u>Scintillating</u> writing, Lucas, truly

-0:10:06 Artoo is using Kenobi's hand-held commlink. This is true for Threepio in <u>A New Hope</u> as well, way back (um, forward?) in the Death Star. Why do droids need hand-held commlinks? Why don't they have onboard tuners?

-0:10:21 Anakin's hanging in the elevator shaft. Why don't the droids just <u>shoot</u> him? (Please?)

-0:12:55 Continuity, the stupidly named Count Dooku on the steps

-0:13:10 Dooku Force-lifts Kenobi. Lucky he didn't behead Obi-Wan while he had the chance, huh?

-0:14:30 Um, don't look kids, somebody's hands just got cut off

-0:16:10 The ship fell for eight whole seconds before somebody thought to call out "reverse stabilizers!" They all busy reading comics, or something?

-0:16:49 Look at the design on the emergency booster engines. They're pointed at the ship itself. How can they provide lift?

-0:16:52 Continuity, leveling out the ship

-0:17:25 Our heroes grapple onto I-beam. This shaft didn't <u>have</u> I-beams in it earlier

-0:17:30 Continuity, elevator escape—they swing through the doors twice

-0:17:43 Yay, Artoo has those cool <u>jets</u> he can use to get out of trouble...

Sigh...

-0:17:58 Ray shields? What? I guess Lucas can make up whatever crap he wants, but why do these not appear at any other point in all six movies?

-0:20:11 It's a laser sword, guys—wanna be a little more careful when you cut handcuffs off somebody?

-0:20:18 "Run!" This is from a droid. Since when do robots retreat?

-0:20:36 Continuity, Kenobi's lightsaber

-0:20:40 Broken <u>glass</u>? On a <u>starship</u>? What happened to Star Wars brand transparisteel?

-0:20:43 Continuity, Grievous

-0:21:26 From the outside, the escape pod is spinning. Cut inside...no spin!

-0:22:37 Boy, this imminent crash would be more exciting if I cared

-0:23:12 Did Anakin fly the burning hulk right to a landing strip, or are they all just really lucky one happened to be down there?

-0:23:51 Watch for a YT-1300 freighter (maybe it's the <u>Falcon?</u>) down lower left

-0:24:13 Continuity, Kenobi's hair

-0:25:36 Ah, good old <u>reflective</u> Threepio

-0:26:14 Since Leia's mother died in childbirth, and she never knew her (comments in <u>Return of the Jedi</u> notwithstanding,) what are the odds that they would do their hair in a similarly doofy way?

-0:26:28 Padme made a huge deal about how their relationship is supposed to be secret. So...why are a Jedi Knight and the former queen of Naboo kissing in public? Are there no paparazzi on Coruscant?

-0:28:44 Does Grievous not know Palpatine is Sidious? They were just on the ship together—I'm so confused

-0:29:56 I've never had curly hair so maybe I'm wrong. But does it make sense to put a brush through curls? Doesn't that...de-curl them?

-0:31:37 Padme wears pearls to bed...that must be comfy

-0:36:53 "Allow this appointment lightly the council does not." Sigh...the movie is confusing enough without trying to translate Yoda

-0:37:00 Am I the only one that finds a hologram sitting in a real chair a bit goofy?

-0:37:53 Am I the only one that finds a hologram <u>looking around</u> as though he's in the room a bit goofy?

-0:39:16 Continuity, Kenobi

-0:40:56 "I hope right you are." Aaaaagh!

-0:42:18 Continuity, Padme and Whiny

-0:43:01 Cameo right here in the opera house hallway, of Lucas and his daughters—only time George appears in any Star Wars film

-0:47:00 Palpatine dangles "resurrect the dead" carrot in front of Whiny. Why would he do that? Did Anakin tell him about dreaming that Padme died? Are they that close? Or, creepier, does Palpatine have the happy couple's bedroom bugged?

-0:49:43 Well it's about time we saw a Wookiee battle!

-0:52:18 Kenobi's starfighter/hyperspace ring zip off into lightspeed, and the buoys left behind bob up and down...are they in water? It's outer space!

-0:54:00 Ring comes out of hyperspace, Kenobi backs the ship off and then...flies through the ring. Careful, Obi-Wan! Break that ring and you're stranded out here!

-0:57:45 Continuity, lightsaber

-0:57:58 Earlier when Kenobi was on the bridge of Grievous' ship, he decapitated a big droid—which proved useless as said droid kept coming. Now he's facing the exact same type of robot, and he does the same thing, cuts its head off! Guy never learns

-0:58:05 Lucky for Kenobi that Grievous doesn't just let the minions shoot him

-0:58:57 Grievous has four lightsabers and he still can't connect on Kenobi?

-0:59:00 So you might ask yourself why this robot-thing has Force powers. Well, I'll tell you what Lucas told me, or at least what he said on the DVD commentary: apparently at some point in the past, General Grievous received a blood transfusion from a Jedi...and bango! Force user!

So all a person who wants Force powers need do is get blood from a Jedi! Pass it on!

-0:59:15 Continuity, two remaining sabers

-0:59:53 Continuity, Grievous

-1:00:03 Why does Kenobi not use the Force against Grievous as the bad guy goes for his vehicle? Or throw something at him, or…

-1:01:02 Huh. The separate holograms <u>look</u> at each other. How does <u>that</u> work?

-1:01:45 "The dark side of the Force surrounds the chancellor." So why do you Jedi folks send Whiny to be alone with him? Knowing all about the anger issues he has?

-1:03:04 Continuity, Palpatine and Whiny

-1:04:56 "The Jedi know no emotion, only peace." This may be Jedi philosophy, but it doesn't lead to a balanced life. Emotions cannot be escaped, and denying such things as anger, grief, etc. just denies basic needs

-1:05:20 I question the physics on the giant rolly-wheel <u>turning</u>

-1:05:39 Continuity, rolly-wheel chase

-1:06:31 Continuity, fight on the balcony

-1:06:51 Continuity as Grievous throws Kenobi

-1:07:09 "Shot through the heart, and you're to blame…" Why does the General's blastered heart catch <u>fire</u>? No, wait, why does the <u>robot</u> have a <u>heart</u> in the first place?

-1:10:00 Why does the whole council take off to see Grievous' dead body? Besides the fact that Skywalker is conveniently left alone?

-1:11:29 Wow, saber right through him. PG-13, huh?

-1:11:30 Continuity, sabered Jedi. And why doesn't the other gal take a swipe at Sidious while she has the chance? Oops, too late—well, continuity issue as she dies, too

-1:12:30 Remember back (well, forward) when Kenobi was all "If you strike me down, I shall become more powerful than you can possibly imagine"? Why don't the other Jedi get to be all ghosty and give advice? Or would things get too crowded?

-1:12:34 Again with the glass! Way up high in the air!

-1:13:46 Dark side aging very well done (said without sarcasm) and not at all too much for PG-13 rating (sarcasm on that one)

-1:13:58 Seems like Windu could do something besides just stand there

-1:14:20 "He must stand trial!" Why? Grievous didn't, Maul didn't, Dooku didn't

-1:15:35 "Become my apprentice. Learn to use the Dark side." And you too can look like the Cryptkeeper

-1:20:22 Lucky Commander Cody (! Really?) is still alive to give Kenobi his lightsaber back

-1:20:42 Commander Cody (never get tired of that name) looks at a hologram in his hand. His projection over in Palpatine's office isn't looking at his hand. Why not?

-1:20:58 Why is Kenobi riding along a sloping cliff with his saber ignited? Isn't that dangerous?

-1:21:03 Sure is lucky he landed in the only pool of water on, like, the whole planet. Should have died anyway, falling from that height—must've used the Force to save himself somehow

-1:22:00 Yoda looks unhappy, as though he were grieving the many Jedi deaths. Why? Back at 0:34:20 he told us all that there is no emotion but peace for a Jedi

-1:23:48 Remember cute little Anakin, the podracer? He just slaughtered a bunch of defenseless children! Could I hate this movie more? Damn you, George Lucas!

-1:24:09 Padme breaks down in tears. Is this some preggo hormone thing? She shouldn't know about the current Jedi pogrom, should she?

-1:25:15 And Kenobi's okay! He's not even minorly injured! Wow!

-1:25:51 And of course <u>Chewbacca</u> is one of the two Wookiees with Yoda. Out of all the Wookiees on Kashyyyk. Surprised a young Han Solo isn't around someplace

-1:27:09 Okay, I'm confused again. I could probably go back to the last shot of the ship Kenobi arrived in, but I hate this movie so I don't wanna. Kenobi and Grievous fought to the death on this platform, and now Kenobi jumps in the ship to leave the planet. This is the ship Grievous was heading for.

So here's the question: whose ship is it? If it's Kenobi's, what did Grievous plan to do with it? If it's the General's, how does Kenobi get in so easily, and how lucky is it that the controls don't require four arms?

-1:29:30 Crew reflection in Artoo's shiny dome. Wave, fellas!

-1:31:15 There are droids all over this galaxy, why are living creatures scooping the magma on Mustafar? And could the platforms they use for such <u>be</u> more unstable?

-1:32:18 "If a special session of Congress there is, easier for us to enter the Jedi temple it will be." For the love of all that is holy...if he weren't 900 years old and a Jedi Master, I swear I would kick Yoda in the butt

-1:32:16 Continuity, Yoda the dangling participle Master

-1:32:40 The Mustafar lava field is pretty cool. Too bad the rest of the film sucks

-1:33:18 Why are the little droids running in <u>terror</u>? Who keeps giving droids the ability to feel emotion? (If anything should feel nothing but peaceful, it would be a robot...)

-1:34:17 The Jedi have kept the peace for hundreds, maybe thousands of years. Far as I am aware, in this universe they have been well-respected and honored and looked-up-to. Or have they? Because right here Palpatine talks about one rebellion, offers no proof to back his claims...and suddenly poof! The Jedi are disfavored. Just like that

-1:34:30 Well, at least Anakin was nice about it. Five light sabered children on the floor—no missing limbs

-1:35:30 Anakin rampages around on Mustafar. There are droids with guns in the room—why are none of them firing upon him?

-1:35:31 Continuity, lightsaber

-1:37:20 Security recordings are holograms? Does that make sense?

-1:37:35 Palpatine allows Jedi-accessible security cameras in his <u>office</u>?

-1:38:30 Seems a huge waste of power to just keep a ship "parked" in mid-air like that

-1:43:05 Crew reflected in shiny Threepio

-1:43:50 Huh. I thought somebody in their final trimester wasn't supposed to fly. Maybe that doesn't apply to starships?

-1:44:11 Annie's eyes were all Darth Maul-ish not long ago. Now they're not. Why?

-1:44:47 Padme has one hand on Anakin's face, shot changes and magically she's got both hands on his face

-1:46:11 Continuity, Anakin

-1:47:50 Continuity, lightsaber battle

-1:48:49 Palpatine tosses Yoda straight for a wall, shot changes and the little green guy hits two feet to the right of where he was just pointed

-1:49:45 Lucky for Yoda that Sidious didn't finish him off while unconscious

-1:49:58 Continuity, Darth Sidious

-1:51:13 Continuity, conference room battle

-1:51:54 Is this a demonstration battle? Kenobi and Anakin pass up a great many opportunities to sever limbs or do damage to each other

-1:53:15 Darth Sidious Force-moved several pods out of his way. Now Yoda gets one spinning and Sidious is suddenly helpless against it. Just because it's spinning?

-1:54:40 Continuity, battle on the pipe

-1:55:40 No nit, just a thought—this fight seems like it goes on for hours

-1:56:11 Caught this even in the theater, first time around—a piece of factory hits the lava and Kenobi's blade is pointed down. Shot changes and it's up

-1:56:46 "Into exile I must go." I can't help you with your troubles, I have to run off for twenty years. Tell Luke I'm on Dagobah if he ever gets off Tatooine, will ya?

-1:56:58 Kenobi and Vader cling to the structure—seems like either could pull off the other with the Force, but it doesn't seem like either is trying to

-1:58:00 Ooh, new set piece for this never-ending battle. Now they're on little platforms!

-1:58:30 I don't know if this is a nit or not—Kenobi's eyes look dilated

-1:58:31 "Anakin, Chancellor Palpatine is <u>evil</u>!" Um, didn't Kenobi say earlier in this very film that "only Sith deal in absolutes?"

-1:59:52 "You were the chosen one!" Yeah, about that—nobody ever explains how the prophesy went all wrong, and while I'm asking, what's with that midi-chlorian nonsense?

-2:00:47 Will Award. I'm still mad about this and the movie came out, like, four years ago. Anakin's on fire, screaming, writhing. The lava damage, the need for his new robotic body could have easily been implied. None of this needed to be shown. Nobody's impressionable young children needed to have nightmares of this moment.

Shame on you, Lucas.

-2:04:29 Vader's broken body in a medical hoverbed—with no cover over it. Bet the rain feels good on those burns, huh?

-2:05:23 Apparently Vader gets a longer leg upgrade at some future point—he sure ain't seven feet tall in this shot

-2:06:03 Um, why is a <u>droid</u> delivering the babies? No human doctors available on Coruscant?

-2:07:58 Wow that's a nice voice synthesizer inside the Vader helmet! Whiny sounds just like James Earl Jones!

-2:09:15 Take the kids someplace that Vader won't find them. Like—yeah, how about Tatooine? Where Vader grew up? He'll never think to look there!

By the way, keep your ears open as Kenobi hands baby Luke over to hear 11 notes of the <u>Harry Potter</u> theme— a little Easter egg from John Williams

-2:11:10 Twenty years from now all the ships will be new, the equipment will look different—and just to prove the Empire has no fiscal responsibility, they apparently throw all the previous models away...because we <u>never</u> catch sight of any of this stuff ever again!

My head hurts. Can I leave this galaxy now? Please?

#23:   Terminator II

Ruminations: Note the First: this is the movie
replacing Inception, which is not in this Volume for reasons
explained in the Foreword

Now this is a movie that changed my life. (No,
really.) Being only thirteen when this came out--and being
raised by very caring parents--I never saw R-rated T2 in
theaters, but I certainly heard about it, and when the movie
finally played on local television I had my VHS player ready. In
fact, the prime-time "edited for content" version was the only
version I had for some years, and I wore the tape out
watching the movie over and over. The most significant effect
on my life: between my best friend's motorcycle in high-
school and the Harley-Davidson Fat Boy that Arnold drives
around in Terminator 2...I caught a serious case of Cycle
Fever, from which I have not yet recovered. In the past ten
years, I have racked up over 60,000 motorcycle miles on my
Honda Shadow, and rode 1,000 of those miles in one 24-hour
period to become a member of the Iron Butt Association
("World's Toughest Riders"). And all thanks to the incredibly
cool Harley in Terminator 2.[2]

Note the Second: There are no timecode numbers
because at the time of this review, I didn't have the movie on
DVD. (A problem which has since been rectified.) So since no
DVD, I used my PSP to watch the movie on UMD. OK?

---

[2] And as of 2013 I now have a black Harley-Davidson Fat Boy.
Living the dream

Note the Third: same problem here as in <u>E.T.</u> Neither the T-800 or the T-1000 is human--and I don't even want to <u>know</u> if either is anatomically correct--but I'm still going to say "<u>he</u> throws the biker through the window" instead of "<u>it</u> throws the biker through the window" because that would just be weird.

Away we go!

-At this point in time (ha ha) we have been treated to four Terminator movies and a television show featuring robots sent back in time. (I've heard of plans for two more movies.) When are those humans in the future going to figure out they need to destroy the time-portal so that Skynet can't keep sending killer robots back to try and change history?

-In the early future-war montage, a truck fires a missile at the sky ship--it gets hit in front, but explodes from the <u>rear</u>? Also, as battle-worn John Connor surveys the landscape, watch the laser barrage. I'll mark it down to futuristic technology, but the laser beams appear to <u>curve</u> as they fly, and as far as I know, that shouldn't be possible.

-In the early future-war montage, the truck firing the rocket changes positions between shots. Also there are moments where the shiny robots should be reflecting laser bolts but do not. Then the sky ship falls out of the sky twice!

-So the Arnold-lookalike T-800 and the Robert Patrick-looking T-1000 arrive on the same night, just minutes apart. We aren't given a whole lot of information about the circumstances under which both are sent back in time, but since we're talking time travel, it would sure make a lot of sense for the T-800 to come back a month or a year before the 1000 does. It would ruin the movie, but...

-For whatever reason, the Terminator writers decided that when you get sent back in time, you go back naked. It's my understanding this is because only living material goes back. But wait--your hair, your nails and the outer layer of your skin are dead tissue...how come they go too? (Because if they didn't it'd be <u>really</u> gross!)

-If it's true that only living cells go back, how does the liquid-metal T-1000 show up at all?

-I have many issues with the T-800's "robot vision". He's a cyborg from 40-some years in the future, so I'll allow that maybe the three- and five-digit number lists and the motorcycle designation codes have some function that I don't understand. However, I don't know why the display only registers make/model types for most of the cycles ("Model 435 Harley-Davidson," "Model 236 Yamaha") and yet pulls up "Electro-Glide" (sic). Then the last bike registers as a "Fat Boy" but not as a Harley. (I would expect the display to be consistent.)

-This made me laugh. A lot. For a super-intelligent cyborg from the future, at least one of the T-800's files is corrupt: the display over one of the Harleys reads "Electro-Glide"...it <u>should</u> read "Electr<u>a</u>-Glide".

-Well, <u>I</u> learned something: the designations the 800 applies to the people in the bar (ENDOMORPH, ECTOMORPH, MESOMORPH) all refer to different body-types. (I looked it up.) What gets me, though, is how it can just <u>look</u> at a female and conclude she's 5'1" and 98 pounds.

-According to the 800's heads-up display, the barfly who meets his needs is a 99% match. This is pretty accurate: the display says that the dude is 6'1" and 212 pounds. However, assuming the T-800 is modeled after the 1985 Arnold Schwarzenegger we all knew and loved, the T-800 is

6'2" and 235 pounds. Seems like his clothes would be just a little snug, don't it?

-The T-800 throws the guy whose clothes he needs onto the grille in the kitchen, and supposedly it's burning the dude. However, the steam jets under the bar's grille are quite visible.

-What luck for the T-800! The guy who owns the Fat Boy that he has decided would be the perfect vehicle is also a match clothing-wise! How efficient! Of course, I don't know how the 800 could tell by <u>looking</u> at the guy which bike was his...

-Um, how do I put this delicately...the T-800 walks into the bar stark naked, and walks out in new-to-him biker duds. Did he also take the biker's <u>underwear</u>? Or is the 800 going <u>commando</u>? (These are the kinds of questions that keep a nitpicker up at night.)

-Why exactly is a cyborg from 2029 modeled after a guy from 1985, anyway?

-The bar owner comes out with a shotgun and tells the 800 that he can't let Arnold take the guy's wheels. (He didn't keep the cyborg from taking his patron's <u>clothes</u>, but anyway...) The T-800 puts out the kickstand, leans the bike over, gets off, slowly advances on the bar owner...did the owner not <u>see</u> that this guy just shrugged off a knife-stab, then easily tossed a man his size into the next room? Dude, start shooting!

-The T-800 advances on the bar owner and stops. Then the shot changes and instantly Arnold is about a foot closer.

-As the T-800 grabs the shotgun from the bar owner, his hands on it change position between shots.

-Is there a logical reason for this <u>robot</u> to grab a pair of sunglasses? Yes, he looks much cooler...is looking cool one of his mission parameters? (Apparently, as the peel out from the bar isn't necessary either, and increases the risk of an accident.)

-This is just me, but I feel that sticking a loaded, cocked shotgun between the tailpipes of a motorcycle isn't an especially clever thing to do.

-While on the subject, I have to question the 800's choice of a Harley-Davidson motorcycle as ideal. Hey, I'm glad he picked that vehicle (see Ruminations,) but what are the criteria of the mission? Find John Connor and protect him. Try to keep a low profile. Knowing that another future cyborg is around who wants to kill John, why pick a motorcycle? You can't hide the kid's presence, it's not the safest vehicle in the best circumstances, it's very noticeable--and the T-800 should anticipate that they're going to be involved in high-speed chases, shootings...

-This movie obviously was released before California's motorcycle helmet law went into the books. (In 2004, I tried to ride less than one block in CA without the benefit of my helmet, and two different drivers honked and signaled me about it. No way the 800 could remain inconspicuous and un-ticketed without one.)

-The T-1000 comes into the world with a burst of electrical discharge, which is noticed by a LA police officer, who then drives up to take a look. There are huge arcs of electricity flying around, and he drives up to take a look?

-The T-1000 doesn't need to wear clothing like the 800, it just makes clothing out of his liquid-metal self. For some reason, however, the T-1000 stays in Robert Patrick mode as much as possible. Why not just switch identities with whoever you are trying to be? (I'm sure Robert Patrick would have some problems with this idea.)

-The T-1000's keystrokes in the cop car don't match the display.

-As the T-1000 manipulates the police computer, we learn that J.M.A. stands for Juvenile Automated Index. Does that seem right?

-I'm going to save most of my going-back-in-time ranting for <u>Back to the Future</u>, but I can't let this go: how...in the world...is it remotely conceivably possible that John Connor could send a soldier back in time to become <u>his own father</u>??

-Doc Silberman, speaking of Sarah Connor: "She stabbed me in the kneecap with a pen three weeks ago." Boy, he's recovered well, no limp at all!

-When step-father Todd comes out of the house to yell at John, he descends the first step twice.

-As the T-1000 tries to find John, and is forced to be nice to people, we see that his "personality" module is very impressive. Much less robotic than the 800...obviously upgrades were made! (Or perhaps Robert Patrick is a better actor than Arnold. Take your pick.)

-The T-800 drops by John's house before the T-1000 does. (As John's stepfather talks to the 1000, he says "There was a big guy on a bike here earlier.") One wonders what the T-1000 was doing all night, since it had John's address almost immediately upon arriving.

-As Dyson goes into the cyborg-leftover room, the people around him are in clean suits...but he's not, nor is the security guard. Huh?

-As Dyson goes to get the leftover cyborg arm, the security-guard makes a big deal about how the keys to unlock the cyborg-artifact room must be turned <u>together</u>. He counts down "three, two, one,"...but Dyson and the security-guard still don't turn the keys at the same moment.

-The security guard's lips are out of sync as he says "three, two, one, turn."

-The security guard must be new, or must not really care about Dyson. He says, "How's the wife and kids?" Dyson only has <u>one</u> child.

-The T-800 is motoring along, trying to get lucky and pick up John somewhere in L.A. Movie fortune is with him, as suddenly he snaps his head around and registers John and friend on the motorbike. He looks around <u>before</u> he sees the bike. He hears a motorbike's engine and <u>knows</u> it's John Connor somehow?

-As the T-800 sees John on his motorbike, the heads-up display registers, among other things, "lateral speed". The speed at which the cycle is going from side to side? What possible use would this information be?

-Also, is there some computer-related breakthrough in the next twenty years that invalidates binary code? Why does the T-800's heads-up display print English words?

-When the T-800 finds John riding his motorbike, the tracking shot of John on the display doesn't work with how far Arnold's head is turned. He shouldn't be able to see the kid anymore.

-The T-1000 talks to a <u>very</u> young Nikki Cox about where Connor might be. Her lips don't match the audio.

-John heads to the mall with his stolen money, and we catch up with him at the arcade. It's a <u>very</u> clever moment that this child, upon whose life or death the future of the world hinges, is playing a game where the player tries to keep nuclear missiles from destroying a city. But honestly, <u>I</u> was thirteen in 1991 and no way would I have been playing <u>Missile Command</u>. (Apparently John really likes the classics.)

-Supposedly the 800 hides his shotgun in the box of roses he's carrying--but the box of roses has a clear window (you can see the roses) and there's no shotgun in there. Also, did the 800 steal the roses? Where'd he get money with which to buy them?

-It seems a little convenient that the back door to the arcade wasn't locked, and wasn't an Emergency-Exit-Alarm-Will-Sound type of door.

-Again, the T-800 exhibits a little too much advanced knowledge: he points his shotgun at the corner where the 1000 is going to appear, though I can't imagine how he knew the guy was coming.

-In addition to his fancy shape-changing tricks, the T-1000 can also manufacture bullets! In the mall's back hallway, he fires twenty-four shots without reloading from a gun that can hold, at most, thirteen rounds.

-You can see the bumps under the 800's jacket as he shields John in the hallway--bumps that become bullet holes as the squibs go off.

-As the T-1000 fires his 24 shots, some of the shots go off without accompanying flashes.

-When Arnold turns around, there are no holes in his front, but later when John holds up the t-shirt the 800 was wearing, there are holes straight through.

-Follow along now, in the back-hallway battle: Arnold fires the shotgun the first time. Cut to the 1000: two visible shotgun holes. Arnold shoots a second time. Now there's three holes. A third blast. There's still three holes. A fourth blast. Now there's five holes. A fifth blast, and there's still only five holes. The sixth and final blast...and now there's seven holes!

-Remember, now: the 1000 didn't put on the policeman's clothes, he just made them out of his liquid-metal self. It is therefore rather impressive to realize that out of his own "flesh" the 1000 manufactured a badge, a nameplate, and even a pen! As the holes from the 800's shotgun blasts close, the 1000 goes to the trouble of re-establishing these things. He is definitely into his character.

-It's a very nice touch that the T-1000, as he passes through the clothing boutique, stops for a second to look at a silver mannequin...but it makes no sense that this robot would pause in his mission to do such a thing.

-You don't even have to freeze-frame the dirt-bike jump as John Connor leaves the mall to see that it's a stunt double on the bike.

-The T-1000 chases John on his bike, and commandeers a big tow-truck. At one point, the truck slams into a car and you can see the car has no driver.

-During the chase in the canal, it's lucky that the T-1000 decided to toy with John first, hitting the bike then backing off, giving the 800 time to come to the rescue.

-As John careens his motorbike through the canal, water is splashed onto the lens several times.

-Right before the tow truck plows off the bridge, John looks down the canal--there's printing on the bridge that says "Hayvenhurst Ave", but a very obvious sign behind the truck as it hits that same bridge says "Plummer".

-There's lots of things wrong with the tow-truck crashing into the canal and subsequent chase. The front grille falls off during the crash, the axle breaks, a window falls out...yet the window, the axle and the front grille all repair themselves.

-It's very obviously a stuntman on the motorcycle during the jump into the canal, and the film is very obviously sped up just after. You see more of this stuntman in subsequent shots as the 800 passes the tow truck.

-Fun one: John's motorbike falls back onto its <u>left</u> side, but as the wheels of the tow truck go over it, it's lying on its <u>right</u> side.

-Arnold points his shotgun at the tow truck's engine, but somehow the round twists sideways and under and blows out the truck's <u>front tire</u>.

-Freeze frame the truck destruction and watch the dummy in the front seat!

-There are a few glitches as the T-1000 walks out of the flames in his silver form.

-I know the T-800 is from the future, but it seems fantastic and <u>ever-so-slightly</u> unbelievable that his technology allows living tissue to be draped over a metal skeleton in such a way that the tissue can live for long periods. (Like, years and years.)

-It always amazes me to watch movie characters ride motorcycles around at high speeds without eye protection of any kind. Believe me, if you're riding a motorcycle at <u>any</u> speed over about 30 MPH without glasses/goggles, you can't see a <u>thing</u>. (And your hair doesn't stay nicely in place, either)

-The 800 robot smashes a phone to get the coin John needs to call home--before he does so, take a look at the phone...it already looks rotted away.

-John's talking about his psycho mother while the T-800 stands a few feet away, monitoring the area. Then after a closeup of John, we see them both...and between shots the T-800 has moved several feet closer without making a sound.

-Eddie Furlong, who plays John Connor in this movie, was going through puberty during filming. The film was shot out of order, so his voice and his height go up and down during the course of the movie.

-I was impressed that the T-1000 could make a pen? When he takes the place of John's stepmother, his disguise extends to her frizzy, curly <u>hair</u>! All made out of his liquid-metal flesh! Incredible! (He also goes to the trouble of making a wedding ring, and making it metallic, so it catches the light.)

-Not that I'm complaining, but there's not a whole lot of blood when the T-1000 puts his blade hand through stepfather Todd's head. (While I'm on the subject, it struck me on this latest viewing that if the exact same film released today, if you toned down some of the language, it might just earn a PG-13 rating. How the world changes...)

-"So it could disguise itself as a pack of cigarettes." "No, only an object of equal size." Compare Robert Patrick with stepmother Janelle with the Pescadero cop...the "equal size" thing is fudged quite a bit.

-The T-800 is a robot on a mission, and John Connor doesn't know yet that the machine has to obey his commands. Why does the 800 stand there and listen while John tells him his life story? Get moving, people!

-John starts screaming "Help! Get this psycho off me!" and the gas-station dudes hear and react. They're maybe thirty yards away, but it takes <u>forty-five</u> seconds before they're on the scene. Did they go the long way around the gas station?

-So the T-800 is a strict-constructionist? He can only do <u>exactly</u> what he's told? I ask because he stands there with his foot in the air until John tells him to put it down. That action calls attention to himself and likely does not help the mission...but John only told him to stand on one foot, he never said the 800 couldn't <u>stop</u>.

-The gas-station guy in the yellow shirt says something ugly, looking off-screen. It appears that he's looking at the 800, but John reacts like the guy was talking to him.

-Maybe the foot thing has the 800 questioning his role: John says "put the gun down, <u>now</u>!" which is a direct command, but the 800 thinks about it for a second before complying.

-The touch of a <u>boot</u> is enough physical contact for the T-1000 to completely mimic the Pescadero cop? I'm having trouble with that one...

-Sarah Connor is a dangerous, mentally unstable prisoner. So why is there a lock on the <u>inside</u> of her cell? (Because otherwise she couldn't escape, silly!)

-You gotta feel bad for the Pescadero cop. He's destined to be fragged by the T-1000, and right before that happens we learn that he's also kinda stupid. He gets his Poker coffee cup out of the machine, and exclaims, "I've got a full-house!" The cards are as follows: Jack of diamonds, Jack of hearts, Ace of clubs, Ace of hearts. For a full-house, the card on the bottom of the cup would have to be either a Jack or an Ace. It's the Queen of hearts.

-That T-1000 is truly a master of disguises--in addition to making a badge, he also forms an I.D. tag (complete with picture) from his liquid-metal flesh. When he drags the guard into the closet, there's a set of keys on the 1000's belt...but he still grabs the guard's gun after this. So did the 1000 grab the keys but forget the gun, or did he just make a set of liquid-metal keys?

-Seems like the 1000 would have an easier time getting around the mental hospital if he stayed in his Pescadero cop disguise.

-"There's 215 bones in the human body. That's one." Great line. For the record, though, not that Sarah necessarily should have known this, there's only 206 bones in the human body.

-John gets off the motorcycle at the mental hospital, and his hair looks <u>amazing</u>. Considering the recent high-speed motorcycle ride...well, whatever he uses for product, I want some!

-The T-800 smashes the gate-booth window, pushes a button without looking and the gate opens. There's four buttons on the panel. First-time lucky?

-Sarah Connor really is strong to just snap a key off in a lock like that. Try it some time--it's not all that easy.

-In a high-action scene Sarah breaks out of her cell, takes down a couple guards, grabs Doc Silberman to use as a hostage, fights her way to freedom...and then stands in the hallway WAITING FOR THE ELEVATOR???

-Apparently they don't pay their female guards enough at Pescadero. Everybody swarms the 800 robot, and he pushes the woman away (why he treats her lightly just because she's a woman doesn't make much sense--he's a robot, what does he care?) She's not unconscious or disabled, and yet she never comes back into the fight.

-The T-1000 really likes his morphing effects, doesn't he? He likes the look on people's faces. That's the only explanation I have as to why he bothers taking the time to morph through the barred door, giving our heroes a chance to run for it, rather than just <u>shooting John</u> from the other side. He's got a gun, he's got bullets, he's got a clear shot.

-You thought the mall hallway was bad: as the T-1000 chases our heroes towards Pescadero's elevator, he fires <u>twenty-six</u> times without reloading, from a gun that only holds thirteen rounds.

-The shotgun-blast-to-the-head effect is really great...but if you freeze-frame right <u>before</u> the gun fires, you can see that the damage is already done.

-As our heroes escape from the T-1000 in the mental hospital <u>elevator</u> (is there something <u>wrong</u> with the stairs in this place?), I kinda think that after the first time the metal sword poked through the ceiling, I would get as flat on the floor as I could possibly manage. John and Sarah just kinda crouch.

-The trip down in the elevator takes almost a minute...just how high <u>is</u> this building? Seems far too long.

-Our heroes aren't immune to the need for magic bullets: as they back away from the T-1000 in the police car, Sarah fires at the machine thirteen times--from a gun that only holds eight bullets. After she changes clips, she gets it right, and only fires eight shots before "I'm out."

-The T-800 fires his shotgun twice without a cocking sound in-between.

-The pistol wounds the T-1000 takes during this chase don't correspond to the shots fired.

-Even robots care about their appearance. The T-1000 manages to barely latch onto the back of the police car as our heroes take off, and he is then dragged along the road for a short while. However, when he gets up to the trunk and starts breaking into the car, there is no trace of road rash. He must have wiped that off right before we see him!

-Freeze frame the moment the T-1000 breaks the back window of the police car, and you'll see that it breaks before he hits it.

-The rear-projection during the dialogue in the police car is pretty obvious.

-"Why do you cry?" Is the 800 just making conversation? He says later that he has "detailed files" on human anatomy. There's no entry in those files on 'tears'?

-To further my incredulity at the technology that allows living flesh on a metal body, the 800 even has <u>healing</u>

capabilities. I'm goggled at the very thought. (Goggled, I tell you!)

-Kinda stupid for the 800 to break the driver's window of the station wagon without checking to see if any of the doors were <u>open</u> (which the passenger side was)

-Car keys in the visor? I <u>refuse</u> to believe anybody ever does this!

-John's position changes between shots as the T-800 says "Affirmative" and then John starts giving him a hard time about how robotic he sounds.

-Our heroes head south, and Sarah warns the 800 to watch himself because they don't want to get pulled over. (Does it make sense that the robot is driving? I know I'm something of a control freak, but I would have a hard time with that, myself.) Considering the way the 800 almost head-ons into a semi truck as they pull into the hamburger joint, <u>somebody</u> really should teach the robot some driving rules.

-"It's in your nature to destroy yourselves." Deep Thoughts, by the Cyberdyne model T-800, utilizing his Soapbox Talking User Personality Interface Directive.

-When did they stop and get Arnold a new jacket? During the hamburger joint scene, I notice that all the holes are gone.

-Sarah starts talking about Cyberdyne, and Dyson, and the 800 says "I have detailed files" with a I-know-where-this-is-going kind of look on his face. A <u>robot</u> with a knowing look on his face.

-Another quick rant on time traveling. The microprocessor from the back-in-time T-800 is being used by Cyberdyne to build the <u>original</u> T-800? But how can an 800 come back in time if the 800 can't be built until an 800 comes back in time? (I'll move on. But I feel better.)

-"Uncle Bob?" And the <u>robot</u> has a problem with being called Uncle Bob because...?

-Nobody seems to mind that this big stranger picks up the baby and peers closely at it. I would think Mama would be just a little concerned, especially knowing Sarah Connor.

-As the 800 and John work on the truck, John's hair changes between shots.

-The T-800 keeps practicing his human-like emotive skills, and he's getting better. Like the excited smile the <u>robot</u> favors us with upon discovery of the mini-gun. Or saying "please" when he asks for a torque wrench. (And why does a <u>robot</u> need a torque wrench? Can't he <u>tell</u> how much pressure he's applying?) Or how the <u>robot</u> looks annoyed at John at the "too slow" high-five fake out. If you watch, you'll also see the robot <u>blinking</u> on occasion. (By the by--are his eyeballs real flesh too? That would explain the blinking, but would raise other questions...)

-A quick note: Linda Hamilton's acting performance in this movie as a desperate, half-crazed woman on a mission is truly incredible. The emotions on her face as she struggles against her own morals by trying to kill Dyson, knowing that doing so is the greater good...truly marvelous.

-One can't really nitpick a dream sequence, but it is interesting to note that in Sarah's dream, as Commando Sarah looks at herself on the playground, that Playground Sarah hasn't changed, she looks just like she did before all the Terminator business (same job, same haircut) yet she also has a child.

-Something I notice a lot as a nitpicker is what I call "Delayed reaction dialogue." I'll show you by way of explanation: Sarah takes off to kill Dyson. John and the 800 go after her. Some time later, we see John and the robot in the car, and the 800 says "This is tactically dangerous. The T-1000 has the same files I do, and might anticipate this move." Is there a reason why the 800 waited until now, miles down the road, to mention this? Delayed reaction dialogue.

-One of the questions this film raises is whether or not it is justifiable to kill one person and save the lives of many. It's a good question: if the possibility existed for you, dear reader, to go back in time to 1930s Germany and kill Adolf Hitler while he was still occupied painting houses...would you? Knowing that his continued existence would eventually rob 6 million people of their lives? The minds behind <u>Terminator 2</u> seem to think that would be wrong, as John and the 800 deliberately stop Sarah from killing Dyson. The only big difference is that Dyson is good, and his actions will cause inadvertent deaths, while Hitler was evil and those deaths were directly his responsibility.

What do <u>you</u> think?

-The RC car hits Dyson in the toes, which shouldn't be possible unless he's sitting very strangely at his desk.

-Sarah needs to adjust her laser sights. The bullet hits the computer monitor roughly 3 inches above where the sight indicated.

-As Sarah climbs the low wall surrounding the house, she changes positions as the shot changes.

-Watch Sarah as she whips out her pistol and shoots Dyson. She <u>closes her eyes</u>, which does not generally lead to a well-aimed shot! (Sure, it works for Leia in <u>Star Wars</u>, and Dr. Calvin in <u>I, Robot</u>, but still!)

-The 800 proves his robotic status by peeling the skin off his arm. Seems a little extreme, but okay--is it a good idea, though, to get blood into robotic electronics?

-The evening at the Dyson's goes on for some time. Sure is lucky nobody called the cops, what with the pistol shooting and screaming and all...

-I understand why John would lead Dyson's kid away--no child is going to be able to handle the sight of a grown man peeling the skin off his robotic arm--but it seems very unlikely, after all that has happened, that mom and dad would just let this strange boy walk away with their son. Plus, it would sure be nice of John and company to <u>warn</u> this traumatized, about-to-go-into-shock couple what's coming, as the robot takes out a huge knife and begins cutting himself.

-Our heroes invade Cyberdyne, but find themselves locked out of the laboratory. Dyson claims that his key won't work, and the T-800 walks up with a grenade launcher. "Let me try mine." Why, the <u>robot</u>'s getting positively <u>pithy</u> now, isn't he?

-Maybe Arnold's just too pretty to shoot. In a repeat of the scene outside the bar, only on a larger scale, the T-800 stands in full-view, hefting a mini-gun, for 10 full seconds and <u>nobody</u> opens fire. Remember, these officers think this guy's a cop killer.

-Since zero casualties are <u>so</u> important to the Terminator now, it's lucky none of his <u>hundreds</u> of bullet ricochets hurt any officers, ruining that "0.0" casualty rating.

-John uses his previously-established hacking skills to find the passcode for the little door. It seems like a police alert would lock out <u>all</u> codes--and it would be a lot faster just to have the robot smash his way in.

-The T-1000 is late to the party, surveying the damage at Dyson's house, when a call comes in over the police radio, talking about the trouble at Cyberdyne. Funny thing...the 1000 doesn't bat an eye at the mention of

Cyberdyne, but turns his head when he hears the name Sarah Connor. Doesn't the 1000 owe his entire existence to Cyberdyne?

-That's <u>some</u> workstation Sarah is hiding behind, considering how many bullets it stops. (They sure make 'em tough, don't they?)

-I have seen this movie a jillion times, but I never until this last viewing noticed that the broken piece of plastic Dyson is holding over the bomb is a piece from the prototype cell-processor they were creating based on the leftover T-800 fragments. He destroys Cyberdyne with something created because of Cyberdyne...very poetic!

-Yet AGAIN everybody crowds into the elevator. In a combat situation, with a bomb about to destroy a whole upper floor, let's get in an <u>elevator</u>?!?

-I don't know much about human physiology, but it seems wrong that Dyson stops breathing, yet holds on to the heavy piece of plastic for an extra three seconds. (Stellar performance, though!)

-A mobile dummy was used during the scene where the cops fire point-blank at the Terminator. It's a good effect, but you can still tell it's not Arnold.

-For some reason, despite everything that has gone on and the continued belief that this T-800 is the same guy that killed all those cops, the SWAT team gives Arnold yet <u>another</u> chance to surrender. And very few of the shots are head shots, despite the fact that this guy could be wearing body armor (he certainly seems unaffected by the bullets) and he's moving slowly, and his head offers quite a target.

-After dispatching the SWAT team, the T-800 walks out of the doors of the building, weapon in hand, and <u>nobody</u> shoots at him.

-This time it's the <u>SWAT van</u> that has the keys under the visor. <u>Come on!</u>

-Why does the police bike's <u>fender</u> catch fire?

-The cycle lights flash the whole time--until the 1000 drives through the window.

-The hole the 1000 makes in the helicopter windshield comes and goes throughout the chase.

-<u>The Will Award</u>: John and Sarah get into the SWAT van and drive off--and there's a cop <u>right there</u> firing a shotgun at them. How lucky that neither John nor Sarah was hurt during this.

-"Chopper, coming in!" The T-800 turns. "It's him." A: how does he know, and B: would one robot refer to another robot as "him"?

-The T-800 takes out the chopper by slamming it into the back of the SWAT van with accompanying explosion. Sure is lucky neither John or Sarah were hurt when he did this...

-As our heroes are chased into the steel plant, a lot of effects are used to keep the real actors from being in danger--some are pretty easily spotted. (No, I'm not going to give you a list. Do I have to do <u>everything</u>?)

-Our heroes crash into the steel mill and watch the T-1000 freeze solid. Think about it: as the robot inexorably, single-mindedly grinds forward, he breaks his legs off from his frozen feet, puts his hand down for balance, and breaks that off. All this time he's had the same grim I'm-coming-for-you expression on his face. After the hand breaks off, he looks at it wide-mouthed, as if in robot shock. Why would a robot bother with such an expression, and more importantly <u>how</u> was he able to change his expression? He's frozen!

-Time for some praise: the effect as the 1000 explodes, and the subsequent melting and re-forming is <u>very</u>

<u>very well done</u>. So is the writing--our heroes are half-dead and it appears as if the 1000 is absolutely <u>unstoppable</u>!

-If you freeze-frame the moment when the 800 swipes into the 1000's shoulder with the iron bar, you'll see the cut is there before the blow is struck. As this happens, the metal spears the 1000 has been threatening Sarah with are <u>instantly</u> gone.

-The T-1000 pulls the bar out of itself, swings it at the 800 and <u>misses</u>, yet Arnold reacts as if hit.

-As the T-1000 is ramming the girder into the 800 over and over, a shot is reused at least once. Arnold's dummy-double also fairly obvious during this scene.

-Why does the 1000 order Sarah to call to John? Is he just accessing his Sadistic Mode? We've already seen that he can exactly imitate people he's sampled by contact. (Even the outdated T-800 can mimic somebody's voice.)

-The T-1000 is threatening Sarah, she tells him where to get off...and the T-800 is suddenly there to save the day. The robot has taken <u>serious</u> damage by now, but he can still move about <u>silently</u>?

-The 800 saves Sarah from the 1000 and the two robots slug it out. This takes about two minutes, but when the 1000 gets back to Sarah, she has barely moved. This is a battle-hardened, tough mama...she must really have been traumatized.

-Sarah hits the T-1000 with six shotgun blasts, knocking him back to the very edge of the pit...but then she's out of rounds and it looks like the 1000 will win again. She could at least <u>try</u> to run up and push him in, he is right on the edge...

-Sarah shoots the 1000 six times with the shotgun after he goes back into Robert Patrick mode, but only five hits are visible.

-At this point the 1000 accesses his Sadism 3.0 function again, as the <u>robot</u> makes a "no-no" gesture at Sarah.

-John and Sarah start to limp away from the advancing 1000, then stop--but they stop <u>before</u> they can see the T-800 coming.

-If you freeze-frame, the T-1000 is already in his weird flower shape before the grenade hits him.

-Once in the liquid metal vat, why does the T-1000 thrash about as if in pain? He didn't seem to feel the shotgun blasts, or the hit with the metal bar, or being blown to pieces...

-Did nobody call the police? The chase from the Cyberdyne building was well-witnessed to lead to the plant, and surely somebody from the plant would call 911...

-"I need a vacation." The <u>robot</u> says this. Honestly...

-"I'm sorry, I have to go away." "Now I know why you cry." I'm sorry, I'll buy twenty-four shots from a thirteen-shot gun, I'll buy a liquid-metal machine that can "make" frizzy hair, but an EMPATHIC ROBOT?!?

-Earlier it was established that the T-800 had to do whatever John Connor said. Was the 800 lying about that to make the kid feel good? At the end, John says, and I quote: "I order you not to go. I <u>order</u> you not to go!" He never countermands this order, but the T-800 gets on the molten pit elevator anyway.

-Sarah presses the button to lower the T-800 without looking--lucky she got the right one, that could be embarrassing. (Sources tell me she actually presses the Up button anyway)

-So they lower the T-800 slowly and dramatically into the molten pit. Um...how is it that the pit is so hot the 800 burns, but the <u>chain</u> lowering him in <u>doesn't</u>?

#24:   Star Wars V: The Empire Strikes Back

Ruminations: It's interesting--as much as I hate, hate, hate the prequel movies, in a similar way I truly love these classic ones! I had a plastic Millennium Falcon model as a kid, had Return of the Jedi sheets...the classic Wars movies are an indelible memory from my childhood. One can only hope children nowadays are saying the same about Jar-Jar and whiny Anakin. And Artoo's jets, don't forget those.

If you read review #22 (or reviews in other Volumes) you know about Chapin & Luttrell's book. So how'd I do, stacked up against the Nerdiest Nitpickers Ever? (At least where Star Wars is concerned)

Hey, I found twenty-four nits they missed. And since this is one of the classic movies, I had a lot of fun doing so.

"I thought they smelled bad...on the outside..."

-0:02:20 In fact, my first nit they didn't get, and it seems an obvious one: the probe fired by the Star Destroyer comes towards camera rotating clockwise, spinning to the right. Next frame it's moving away from camera, only now it's going counterclockwise. It's still spinning to the right, but we're on the other side now! It should be spinning left! (Yes, it's confusing. I've prepared a flowchart)

Even the Family Guy parody had these two shots just like they are in the original. Yet Chapin & Luttrell totally missed this one!

-0:03:07 The stop-motion animation ain't perfect. But I'm not picking nits here--kudos to the people who used to do <u>real </u>effects, instead of expecting computers to do all their dirty work!

-0:03:58 How crappy are these sensors that they didn't pick up the giant Wampa creature? How bad is Luke's Force ability that <u>he</u> didn't catch it?

-0:04:11 Lucky for Luke the Wampa isn't very hungry

-0:06:14 Continuity, the extras crossing behind Leia

-0:07:01 "I simply mentioned that it was freezing in the Princess' chamber." Our little comedy relief droids! See, Threepio told Artoo that it was cold in Leia's room, to Artoo turned the heat up, and now all her clothes are soaking wet! Ha!

Wait...so the construction of this place requires constant freezing cold temperatures or else the walls melt? Why, then, didn't the Princess leave her clothing in storage bins? Did the roof collapse when the walls melted?

Am I a total nerd for wondering? Oh, right. Okay. Moving on...

-0:07:28 Putting a <u>hand</u> over Threepio's mouth mutes him? Really? You can still hear the robot <u>breathing</u>, after all... (And the robot <u>breathes</u> because?)

-0:07:57 Continuity, rebel troopers

-0:08:18 "Then I'll see you in <u>hell</u>!" This galaxy far, far away has a <u>hell</u>? One that people go to, after they die? What are the odds?

-0:09:05 How'd the Wampa get Luke into that upside-down boots-frozen-to-the-ceiling position, anyway?

-0:09:07 First shot of upside-down Luke, his hands are a foot away from the floor. Cut away, cut back, and now his hands are about six inches closer.

-0:09:57 Luke, you might want to shut the cut-through-anything lightsaber <u>off</u> before running around in the slippery snow...

-0:10:47 Is the Artoo unit <u>worried</u> about Luke? As I've said before, whose bright idea was it to give these robots emotional capacitors?

-0:11:30 Fun fact, that I know now only from listening to the DVD commentary: these shots of Luke, in the blinding, whirling, middle-of-nowhere snowstorm, were filmed from the doorway of the crew's Norway hotel! Mark Hamill looks like he's at the ends of the earth, but he's only out in the street

-0:12:18 "The chances of survival are seven hundred and twenty-five to one." This <u>protocol</u> droid needs a <u>tact</u> download

-0:13:18 Obi-Wan Kenobi, the Jedi Google. Luke's dying in the snow, but Ben offers no help whatsoever besides his Yoda info. (And how does a spirit make audible sounds anyway?)

-0:15:03 Continuity, Solo by his tauntaun

-0:15:26 It was too cold last night for the speeders to function. How, then, did the Imperial probe droid survive? (I have this mental picture of a probe droid with long underwear on...)

-0:15:37 I'm not sure of myself here--you check it out and tell me what you think. There are a number of "inside the snowspeeder" shots in this movie where it looks like the dashboard gauges are completely blank. This is one of those

-0:16:14 "I've found them." Sloppy military discipline. The speeder pilot can currently see only Han--he has no information on Luke's current status. To say "I've found <u>them</u>", indicating more than one, is, as I say, sloppy

-0:16:23 Funny how the snowspeeders don't cast <u>shadows</u>. (Can't believe the nerds didn't pick up on this one!!)

-0:18:00 Eeew, Luke and Leia kissing! They're brother and sister!

-0:18:28 It sure seems like the Hoth command center has a nice, matte painting of a snowfield on the back wall. If that's really what I'm seeing--what Rebel commando had nothing better to do than paint <u>that</u> while everybody else was getting dug in on this inhospitable planet?

-0:20:15 Oy--could Vader's ship <u>be</u> any bigger? Wonder if he lost anything important back at the Mustafar lava field--he sure seems to be compensating for <u>something</u>

-0:22:33 So while I listened to the audio commentary, I put up the subtitles to catch the dialogue (though I have this movie pretty much memorized by now.) So I noticed how <u>every</u> time somebody mentioned a Star Destroyer (two words), the subtitles printed "Stardestroyer" (one word.) Check it out at the above timecode, and also 24:13, 37:04, 1:06:07, 1:54:12 and 1:56:23

-0:23:35 Vader talks to General Veers. Is there a video camera on the deck, that Veers is peering into?

-0:25:18 The Rebel ion cannon fires four shots, two of which hit the Stardestroyer (ha ha). Where'd the other two go?

-0:26:00 No nit here—just a kudos to the filmmakers. That AT-AT walker is <u>so</u> deliciously scary!

-0:26:34 More snowspeeders that don't cast shadows

-0:27:01 Speeder opens a drag panel on the right side—which should turn the vehicle right, I would think. Except it turns left?

-0:29:21 I'm not sure why the AT-AT exploded, just because it fell down

-0:30:44 The Rebel speeder driver has red on his face. Which is probably blood—but he's still strapped in. How'd he hit his nose? Or is there a loose pizza in the cockpit?

-0:31:07 Luke is the <u>last</u> of an important race. The last of the Jedi. Why is he out here?

-0:31:09 Continuity, Luke's hands

-0:32:45 Luke grapples up to the AT-AT belly, slashes once with his saber as he dangles—and this nice, neat, four-sided hole opens up. All from <u>one</u> slash?

-0:32:46 Continuity, hanging under the beast

-0:33:00 One grenade and the whole AT-AT explodes? Guys, stop filling those things with C-4!

-0:33:17 The Imperial gives a marker reading: "One seven decimal two eight." Wouldn't <u>point</u> instead of <u>decimal</u> be a tad more efficient?

-0:33:52 Lucky the hallway caving in didn't bury our heroes!

-0:35:36 Stormtrooper continuity

-0:35:37 How did Luke's X-wing get out here? Some pilot get light duty? "Naw, I gotta move that Skywalker fellow's X-wing, I can't go fight the giant Walkers. You go on without me."

-0:36:37 The Rebels need to work on their discipline. What gives Luke the right to just alter course to Dagobah just because he feels like it?

-0:37:17 Say what you will about the Imperials, they put <u>some</u> brakes on their Star Destroyers! They're chasing the <u>Falcon</u>, and in the previous fifteen seconds the Destroyer has traveled, like, fifteen kilometers. Shot changes, and now the huge craft is just barely moving!

-0:37:30 As important as it seems to be to capture the <u>Falcon</u> (I mean, they've got several Star Destroyers on this), there's only <u>four</u> TIE fighters out here? And what about tractor beams?

-0:40:20 Does the <u>Falcon</u> make its own gravity? I suppose it must—nobody's strapped in, yet nobody's floating around the cockpit either. Later on Bespin, when they do that Immelmann turn under Cloud City, the new crew would all be on the ceiling if not!

-0:42:17 Continuity, Skywalker as he turns

-0:42:38 Lucky Artoo can...swim... (is he using those cool jets of his?)

-0:43:40 Lucky Artoo isn't broken after his short flight

-0:45:43 Continuity as Leia falls into Han's arms

-0:46:00 Subtitle nit! As Han says "I didn't have time for anything else," subtitles say "I haven't got time for anything else." Which is a little different

-0:46:16 Nice of the X-wing designers to include a remote cockpit close (wonder if he can also lock the doors with that?)

-0:48:00 The last twenty years sure haven't been kind to Yoda. Must be the weight of his failure back on Coruscant

-0:49:05 "Artoo, let him have it." Luke just gave the droid an order, which Artoo waits awhile before complying with. Sheesh, they sure need the Three Laws of Robotics in this galaxy

-0:52:18 One asteroid, and goodbye Star Destroyer? Maybe these ships aren't so impressive after all

-0:52:25 Ha! Bit of a Freudian slip—right here on the commentary, referring to the Imperials, Lucas calls them "Nazis." We ain't watching Raiders, here, George

-0:53:03 Interesting design on the pad that lights up when Vader's knee touches down. The phone's set up to only dial when he's kneeling?

-0:54:23 Artoo peeks into Yoda's home. Didn't Luke just say "Stay here and guard the camp?"

-0:54:35 Lucky the electronic droid with all the access panels is waterproof

-0:55:35 "I cannot teach him." Sheesh. They've been together for two hours, and Yoda is ready to throw in the towel. Some Jedi Master

-0:55:44 Continuity as Yoda turns to face Luke

-0:56:12 "What know you of ready?" Subtitles: "What know you ready?" Figure Yoda's English is hard enough to understand when you <u>do</u> get all the words

-0:56:35 "This one a long time have I watched." Um...maybe Yoda needs to get the Dish, or something—he has nothing better to do than watch Luke? (Does he see you when you're sleeping?)

-0:57:45 Is there a point to dropping the bombs on the asteroid surface?

-0:58:20 Princess Leia seems fairly well-traveled...she's <u>never</u> heard of mynocks?

-0:59:56 So they landed an entire YT-1300 freighter in this non-cave, and the worm didn't care...but <u>one</u> laser blast and suddenly it's game over?

-1:01:13 What do calisthenics have to do with using the Force?

-1:03:25 The whole fight in the cave is great from a therapy point of view. Seems like most of the time, I'm my own worst enemy. Dunno about you

-1:04:25 All of the land-based creatures seen on Dagobah seem remarkably Earthlike. You know, the snakes, the lizards...very Earthlike, this alien planet

-1:06:08 Why is the Bounty Hunter meeting taking place on the bridge? The <u>Executor</u> not have a green room?

-1:06:23 "I want them alive. No disintegrations." Um...don't Force-choke me, Vader, but someone can be dead and yet not disintegrated

-1:07:44 How did Han back the <u>Falcon</u> up and magnetically attach to the hull without anybody noticing?

-1:08:20 Somebody oughta wipe Artoo off before he starts rusting...

-1:11:13 Sure wish Yoda would explain all that midi-chlorian nonsense from the first prequel movie

-1:12:49 Luke's X-wing was drowned in a swamp for a week—that's gonna hurt the resale value...

-1:13:31 I suppose it establishes how evil Vader is, but what is the point of killing somebody every time they fail at something? They're never gonna learn that way

-1:13:48 The SW nerds noted this too: as the stormtroopers go to pick up recently deceased Captain Needa, drag him off the bridge, it sure <u>looks</u> like the good Captain gives them a little help (watch his legs)

-1:14:54 Continuity, Princess Leia

-1:16:09 Imperial litterbugs! Man, this Empire really is evil!

-1:16:19 Seems like a jittery smuggler like Han would look <u>behind</u> him once in awhile. I mean, Boba Fett's ship is <u>right there</u>

-1:17:05 Yoda tells Luke that if he relaxes into the Force he'll see visions sometimes. And lo and behold, five seconds later Luke is seeing a vision! That was nicely timed

-1:19:36 Yoda Forces the X-wing to rise from the swamp. It majestically floats towards the water's edge, with no landing skids in sight. Cut to a different angle and poof! Landing skids! That Force really is something!

-1:21:44 "She's the fastest hunk of junk in the galaxy." That's the same thing Han always says—so <u>how</u> did the Imperials get here first?

-1:22:54 Somebody take Luke's X-wing down to the body shop? It sure is a lot cleaner than it was last time we saw it

-1:23:02 And just <u>where</u> did the <u>ladder</u> come from?

-1:26:38 Nice shot of the camera guy in super shiny Threepio head

-1:29:32 So Chewbacca, of the sausage-sized fingers, is just gonna throw Threepio back together, huh?

-1:30:05 Seems like a serious design flaw that Threepio's head can be attached backwards

-1:32:00 Nice of the Imperials to leave Chewie something to do, even as he's locked away in a holding cell

-1:34:27 Either the X-wing cockpit got larger (maybe when Yoda magically regrew the landing skids?) or Luke got smaller (all those calisthenics?) because suddenly it's all roomy in there!

-1:35:19 Vader stops Boba Fett from shooting Chewie. Why? Besides the fact that we need Chewbacca for the next movie?

-1:35:57 This is fun, and if you've never heard the story: Han's about to be lowered into the chamber. Leia says "I love you." Han was <u>supposed</u> to say "I love you, too." And Harrison Ford, understandably, thought that was lame. So they thought about it, argued about it, came up with different things to say...and Harrison, last minute, last take, comes up with "I know." Which is the perfect thing for Han to say.

Lucas was not on-set for this, and was reportedly not happy when he heard about it. But it stayed, and good thing, too!

-1:42:19 Chewie must not really be choking Lando. As a practicing martial-artist, I have it on good authority (and personal almost-experience) that if you really cut off the blood flow to the brain, the subject will be unconscious within 5 seconds. I'm not saying Lando isn't uncomfortable—but Chewie must be grieving too much to really get into it

-1:42:48 "Put Captain Solo in the cargo hold." I'm with the Family Guy spoof on this one—where else would you put him? But I'm also surprised at how polite Fett is being. "Captain Solo," indeed?

-1:43:55 How does Luke's saber know to turn itself off when he drops it?

-1:46:08 Seems like, since it's a light source, the lightsaber oughta be reflected in the shiny Vader helmet. Still, the effect has come a long way since A New Hope

-1:46:39 Since Vader wants Luke to rule the galaxy at his side, I guess we're all lucky Luke didn't get sucked out that window to his death

-1:47:27 Well, this is very poorly designed. Information ports and power outlets on Cloud City look so much alike that Artoo can't tell the difference? And he just so happens to have a jack that works in both info ports and power outlets? Bad design both on the droid and on the city...

-1:47:58 Lucky Artoo is Bespin compatible, huh? Are they both running Mac OS-X?

-1:48:17 One frame ago Artoo was plugged into the wall. Then the shot changes and he's unplugged and his dongle has disappeared

-1:48:47 "Ow! That hurts!" This is a droid saying this

-1:52:12 Wow, Luke just fell into a seemingly bottomless shaft. He reached terminal velocity in the first six feet...he'll never survive that. Gonna miss him

-1:52:18 Continuity. Luke gets sucked (lucky him!) into the vent shaft and he's on his face. Shot changes and he's on his back. (Another one Family Guy included in their parody and the nerds missed!)

-1:52:43 Sure lucky that weathervane was there for the grabbing, huh?

-1:53:30 Luke calls out to Ben. Um...what does he expect Kenobi to do, exactly? Catch him?

-1:53:34 Then he calls for Leia. What in the world prompted him to do <u>that</u>? Well—it worked, so good, but still

-1:54:12 "Alert my Star Destroyer to prepare for my arrival." Aside from previously mentioned subtitle nit, why doesn't Vader call his own ship, that really huge one, by its name?

-1:56:14 Another brother-sister kiss...and hey, Han hasn't been gone <u>that </u>long, Princess!

-1:58:24 Escape attempt has <u>Falcon</u> right next to <u>Executor</u>. Why no tractor beams from the Imperial ship?

-1:59:08 Huh. The Imperials unplug <u>one</u> wire and say "Hey, that'll take care of the hyperdrive! They'll never escape!" They don't, like, fry the whole system. One wire.

And another thing: the hyperspace computer plots a course so the ship doesn't hit a star or go through a planet or whatever. (It's not like dusting crops, boy) Lando pulls the lever when the computer says "Go," or whatever, and they don't go into lightspeed. In the meantime, while Artoo is saving the day, the <u>Millennium Falcon</u> ain't pointed exactly where it was. So why do they immediately jump to lightspeed when that one wire is reconnected? Shouldn't the computer have to recalculate?

Or am I overthinking this?

-2:01:20 Saved the Will Award for the very end, and I have to admit—until I saw the Family Guy parody, I never even noticed. But when Lando and Chewie set off to go after Han...Lando is <u>wearing Han's clothes</u>! Which is seriously creepy! He's flying the guy's ship, wearing the guy's clothes, was coming on to the guy's special friend back on Cloud City...

...I don't think Han should trust Lando for a second. Guy's got issues!

#25:   Independence Day

Ruminations: I saw this movie for the first time on August 18th, my eighteenth birthday, at the Tivoli theater in downtown Denver. I chose to spend that afternoon in one of my favorite places: at the movies. Independence Day is truly a popcorn movie: lots of things blow up, the bad guys are scary looking, world-dominating aliens, and only occasionally does the film make any off-handed attempts to relate to real-world issues. You don't leave the show pondering your place in the universe--you walk out with your ears ringing and your heart pounding. Which is just fine by me.

Another note: if movies do really take a page from real life, don't move to New York! Between this movie and Deep Impact, Armageddon, Godzilla, The Day After Tomorrow, War of the Worlds, Ghostbusters...New York is always this close to being destroyed. So do yourself a favor and stay in Tucson, okay?

Note: no timecode on this one. I only had a VHS copy to watch when I did the review. You'll have to forgive me (or not, it's really up to you)

-THERE IS NO SOUND IN SPACE! So how do we hear the rumbling noises as the mother ship goes past the moon? Space is a VACUUM which sound CANNOT travel through.

-As the White House cabinet discusses the approaching aliens, the President says "We may need to upgrade Defcon status." Jumping on his heels, the Secretary of Defense says "The President said to upgrade to Defcon One." No, he didn't. Why isn't this guy already fired?

-We're in New York watching the alien ships come in, and an attractive woman in white is standing arm-in-arm with a suited gentleman on one side of the street. Shot cuts away, cuts back--and suddenly there's all sorts of people around the couple. Did these guys race over from the other side of the street? (Not that I blame them...)

-Cop stops in the middle of the intersection, gets out, looks at the alien arrival...and WHAM! An armored car smacks right into the side of his vehicle, pushing it out of frame. There's no sound of brakes--did the armored car driver not see an entire police car blocking the intersection? (I know--he was on his cell-phone)

-As everybody starts running in panic and the cop on his horse turns to go, he's sideways in one shot, then in the next frame he's straightened out again.

-I go into greater detail about this in my E.T. review (see Volume 4)--but in a nutshell, it's not very logical for we humans to assume that an alien is going to look like us, think like us...have any recognizable features, traits or habits. However, any alien race that visits Earth in the movies invariably has arms, legs, eyes, etc. And in this case, they also have a satellite signal pattern that just happens to correspond to human technology, and is therefore decipherable (and later, exploitable) by us humans! Lucky for us, huh?

-Supersmart David discovers that the alien signal is reducing as it recycles--that in a given time it will be completely gone. Therefore the aliens must be counting down to something, and that something must be evil! (Everybody immediately agrees to this, but it's something of a leap, logic-wise)

-PVP problem: Cap'n Hiller steps out of the house, trips over the kid's toy, picks up the newspaper, looks left (frantic neighbors), looks right (frantic neighbors), a helicopter goes by overhead and only then does he look forward and see a GIANT SPACESHIP hovering over Los Angeles. And this guy is a fighter pilot? The same thing happens to his girlfriend Jasmine when she comes out of the house!

-As David calls his estranged wife, she answers the phone and moves away from the President's press conference, whispering into the phone. Somebody should tell her that a whisper carries a lot further than a low tone.

-As we watch poor Russell Case in the run-down café, the run-down radio is playing a sad, twangy country song. The guitarist playing that song gets stuck on one note, playing it over and over--right as the ground starts to shake because the aliens are coming. It's not a record, it's not skipping...he's just holding on that one note. Strange...

-Captain Hiller comes out to his car, ready to leave for El Toro. Before he can go, he has to pull the little kid out from behind the wheel. Let's look at this: the car is parked on a hill. Jasmine's son is sitting in it, playing around. Does that scenario bother anybody else? (Nobody said Steve or Jasmine was a great parent, but still...)

-The TV general manager: "I gotta call my mother. I gotta call my housekeeper. I gotta call my lawyer...aw, forget my lawyer." We hear him say "forget", but watch his lips. He doesn't say "forget", he says something else entirely. (I'm sure I have <u>no</u> idea what...)

-At the television station newsroom, there's a wall of screens that at one point are showing some twenty-or-so different stations. As David watches the President come on-screen, those twenty individual screens become three big pictures, then finally one giant wall-to-wall picture. Everybody in the building besides David and the station manager are huddled in the basement--who's changing the tv settings? (In addition, as someone who has spent many years working in television, I can tell you that the shot of the President is not a good one. There's no headroom--his head is bumping the top of the screen)

-I love this. Everybody's panicking, trying to get out of D.C. before the aliens attack. We see a wide shot of the parkway...and the two outbound lanes are jammed, while the inbound lanes are empty. Call me crazy, but from what I know of my own kind, <u>all four</u> lanes would be absolutely jammed, along with the shoulder and any drive-able median space.

-"What, you think we'll get to Washington and it won't be there?" Julian is obviously trying to understand what's going on, but David just looks at him goggle-eyed. Wouldn't a <u>little</u> information be nice for the old man?

-As Julian and David drive slowly into Washington, there's a light on Julian's glasses that doesn't move, and which doesn't make sense.

-On the Special Edition DVD, freeze-frame the list of names David scrolls through when he pulls up "Every phone book in America." There are some interesting titles in there, like "Heresheis Avenue."

-By the way, if you really like David's computer and wonder where you can get your own, I'll tell you: you're out of luck. It's a Mac PowerBook, but it's also a prototype that never made it into production. Sorry.

-Ask my fellow television co-workers, and they'll tell you I'm not very technical...but when David "triangulates" the signal to see where his wife is standing in the White House, it seems wrong. For one thing, doesn't triangulation require three sources? (Beyond the technical issues, why is it necessary to do this? Can't they just tell her where they are-- if Connie is so against seeing her husband, why does the triangulation trick win her over?)

-Gotta hand it to Jasmine. When she's in a hurry...she walks off-screen in her, ahem, "work" outfit and then comes back on-screen in street clothes three seconds later. That girl is a quick-change artist!

-Maybe it could be explained as a time delay, but when we cut from the chopper on TV to the chopper in real-life, the lights don't match between shots.

-So to greet the newcomers, the White House sends out a helicopter with fancy lights on it, lights that are setup in a prearranged pattern. Who came up with this pattern, and what in the world is it supposed to do? Demonstrate to the aliens that we have electricity? What makes this special light pattern something the aliens will be able to understand or appreciate?

-The "welcome wagon" starts up the light pattern, and when we're close to the chopper we can hear the lights making "vish, vish" sounds...I've worked with some big lights in my time, and I've never heard a light go "vish."

-So if I understand David's supersmart explanation correctly, the aliens are using our own satellites against us. Are the aliens just too lazy to coordinate their invasion without using Earth technology, or can they not manage the job with their own far-advanced doodads? I suppose that's why these folks have waited since the 50s to invade--they needed <u>us</u> to have a working satellite network first.

-As David says "They're using our own satellites against us," his father disappears, as do the people in the hallway. Alien abductions...

-At first, the countdown timer on the cool Macintosh and the "beep" sounds the computer is making don't match each other. Apparently what David is doing during all the time they sit around in the White House is fixing this--because when he opens the computer in the chopper, at the end of the countdown, the beeps are in synch.

-Everybody runs out to the helicopters and we hear that the rest of the staff will go in the second one...sure is lucky Julian and David found room in that first chopper instead of important White House personnel.

-Okay, here's a really interesting nit: David finally makes the President understand about the countdown, saying "The clock is ticking." At that point the countdown timer is at 28:00:00. The "welcome wagon" chopper goes down, there's a mad scramble for the door, and then as David climbs into the chopper, he opens his laptop and the timer now reads 09:30:00. What in the <u>world</u> have they all been doing for the past <u>eighteen-and-a-half minutes</u>?

-A bunch of happy folks in L.A. are on skyscraper rooftops with signs, partying and ready to welcome the aliens. Is it that easy for the average person to get onto the rooftop of Coit Tower?

-The First Lady runs to her chopper, then stops to look at the loonies on Coit Tower. She looks over, and her eyeline is pointing <u>down</u>, but in the establishing shot, she's much lower than they are. So what is she looking at?

-The aliens really have a flair for the dramatic. One would think that even with their city-destroying superweapon, they would still start the destruction at a city's center point--or if it's <u>that</u> powerful, just pick a spot at random and blast away. But no, they start with Coit Tower, and the Empire State Building, and the White House. And the weapon itself is pretty dramatic--the average H-Bomb does its thing in microseconds, but the aliens' big blaster <u>whooshes</u> through town, blowing apart one street at a time...

    -The ship attacking the White House is apparently fitted with an early model of the alien superweapon--it's the only laser strike that starts a fire, then requires an extra pulse to start things exploding. Hey, wait a minute...<u>why</u> does the White House <u>explode</u>? Are they storing C-4 in the basement, or something?

    -So Jasmine's trying to escape the city in her car, bopping along with the radio...it sure takes her a long time to realize that everybody's running and screaming. And as further proof of just how good a mom she is, once she <u>does</u> realize that the world is on fire, she grabs her <u>purse</u> before her <u>son</u>! (I'm thinking he's going to need some sessions with an alien-invasion surviving psychiatrist later in life.)

    <u>The Will Award</u>: Jasmine fights her way into the tunnel, into the storage closet, the dog jumps in <u>just</u> before the fireball passes...and all three survive. How in the name of all that is holy do they <u>not</u> get fried, hunkering in a small room with an inward-opening door as the full brunt of the alien city-destroying superweapon goes by?

    -Morning of June 3rd, the shots opens on a view of New York, most strikingly the Statue of Liberty's head...which should be pointing <u>away</u> from the direction of the blast, not towards it. Plus the water is remarkably clean considering the city's destruction. (I'm not sure it's that clean in real-life, frankly...)

-At this point we've only lost New York, L.A. and Washington. There should still be, by my reckoning, many military vehicles still available. And with total destruction of three major cities, now we really know the aliens are evil. Yet the first shot of Air Force One has only <u>two</u> planes flying cover. (I would expect a <u>lot</u> more than that.)

-Jasmine and her son walk out of a culvert-type thing into destroyed L.A. It doesn't look like they're walking out of the tunnel they went into...what's the deal?

-Needing transportation, Jasmine finds a truck... I've lost track of how many times some movie character has flipped down a car's visor and <u>poof</u> finds the car keys. I refuse to believe this <u>ever</u> happens in real life, especially in Los Angeles.

-Cut to the pilot wardroom, and the attack briefing. I know it's a common thing to use humor to defuse tension, but these pilots seem to be a little too jovial considering millions of Americans and three major cities have just been obliterated.

-Raven says "We got two on our six," and it's nice of him to notice, because they've been back there, shooting at them, for about thirty seconds!

-In the first stab of the military attack, it sure looks like every pilot fires his number two missile (Sidewinder). Yet Raven establishes that "Damn, they got shields, too!" when he fires his number two missile a <u>second</u> time.

-I find it hard to believe that the military would waste an entire view-screen on the visual display of the airplanes that turns from green to red as they're shot down.

-There's another screen showing what the battle looks like from a top-down view, with graphics indicating where our boys are. Now nobody knew the aliens had personal fighter aircraft--yet as soon as they enter the playing field, that graphic suddenly has alien craft all over it...so whoever designed this thing quickly adjusted the software to reflect the alien craft (complete with accurate design?)

-These alien weapons do strange things. As the alien fighter craft strafe the El Toro tarmac, every laser that hits the field starts a fire, but every laser strike on tarmac does nothing. Furthermore, the aliens either need to adjust their sights or figure out what vehicles are really important-- because as they strafe the runways, not one expensive airplane is hit, only the relatively cheap ground vehicles!

A minute before, Captain Hiller was flying over war-torn Los Angeles. Suddenly he's in a canyon?

-Most consumer automobiles (my former 300ZX included) have a fuel extension--even when the fuel gauge reads Empty, you usually have a few more miles before you're really out of gas. The F-18 must have one of these-- because the gauge reads "000" and yet Hiller flies for another ten seconds.

-It's never explained why the alien craft chasing Hiller finally loses its shield, enabling it to crash. Come to think of it, nobody ever explains why the alien felt it was necessary to chase Hiller all the way to Nevada, either...

-The alien chasing Hiller must have really gotten shaken up in the crash. He pops out of his canopy, all waving tentacles and menace, and one punch from Hiller sends him sprawling. One punch through his bio-exoskeleton. One punch.

-"Sir, they've taken out NORAD." His tone of voice makes it sound like nobody even knew NORAD was under attack. What kind of incompetents are these people? Cheyenne Mountain is really, really important to our national defense. Somebody should have been keeping an eye on it.

-Hiller tells Case that he flew over a military base during his high-speed chase. He must've done this before the canyon bit, which means it was a <u>really</u> long flight. It makes even less sense for the alien to have continued chasing him, too--since the discovery of a hidden military base would probably have been considered much more important than one pilot, yet apparently the alien chasing Hiller didn't tell any of his ugly buddies about it.

-More evidence of military incompetence: the guard at the gate lets Captain Hiller and his unconscious alien through. I can understand that. But why does everybody else in the convoy get to go in as well?

-The report comes in that El Toro has been "completely destroyed." Apparently the aliens got down to business once those dangerous jeeps were out of the way

-It takes a surprisingly long time for the doctor working on the alien body to mention that the creature is conscious, moving around...

-Gung-ho Major Mitchell puts three bullets into the alien's head from about two feet away...and yet there are no bullet wounds.

-Captain Hiller really needs to get his priorities straight. The aliens are kicking our collective butts, we need every available man and all functional equipment--yet he takes an entire helicopter out of service just to go look for his girlfriend. Of course, he is miraculously lucky enough to find the group of seven people in the middle of war-torn Los Angeles.

-David's busy getting drunk, and he pulls a plastic ice tray out of the fridge and bemoans that there's no ice in it. Well why <u>should</u> there be ice in it? It was sitting in the <u>fridge</u>!

-We decide to strike back with a nuclear warhead, and in order to have a visual of what happens, they send out this nuclear-bomb-survivable vehicle. Does such a vehicle really exist? And is this visual really necessary, since establishing shots prove that satellite imagery is still operational?

-When everybody assembles to learn that David can make the alien's shields fail, gung-ho Major Mitchell has to borrow a sidearm from another soldier. What happened to the one he used to shoot the alien earlier? He throw it away in frustration? And isn't this test a little dangerous--David was expecting the bullet to ricochet, but didn't see fit to warn anybody? (I mean, our entire remaining government is in this room)

-A runner up for the Will Award: it is incredibly, staggeringly fortuitous that mankind's computers and the alien's computers are compatible with each other. (Just imagine if all we had were PCs and all they had were Macs...)

-David has the techs remove the clamps holding up the spaceship, and suddenly it floats. This seems wrong. (Plus it's a good thing his computer virus only affected the shields-- that thing would be dangerous if it just fell over!)

-All the remaining pilots gather for a briefing, and Russell Case goes into his "alien abduction" story one last time. The military guys roll their eyes, but given what's happened to the Earth, his story suddenly seems a <u>lot</u> more believable...

-David makes a big deal about tossing his soda can into a recycling bin. I'm thinking that, considering what has happened to most of the Earth, there's very little point in trying to recycle.

-Does the U.S. Government <u>really</u> have Morse Code machines sitting around by the dozen? It's clever, I'll admit, but rather farfetched...

-Perhaps they dug the Morse Code machines out of the same closet that had the Jewish yarmulke! Seriously, where do these things come from?

-World-weary Russell Case struggles into his airplane, pushes one random button...and suddenly a missile is about to launch. I don't buy it. In fact, I'm told it is impossible for a U.S. fighter plane to fire missiles while on the ground due to the Weight-On-Wheels Interlock. So there you go.

-I find it decidedly convenient that the decrepit, broken, crash-landed-in-the-50s spaceship storage bunker happens to have a built-in launch tunnel. Come to think of it, it's also kinda lucky that a human can work the controls-- these aliens have long, seemingly functional tentacles, after all.

-Supersmart David tells Captain Hiller that he expected the mothership would put their craft on autopilot. Why would he expect this? The spacecraft have a manual in it somewhere?

-Gee, I think I mentioned this earlier, but it's weird that the alien ship moans past the camera since there's NO SOUND IN SPACE.

-As David and Captain Hiller sit trapped in the alien mother ship, Hiller freaks out that they can be seen, and David calmly replies, "Power windows," and lowers a blast shield. How did he know that was there? Why doesn't Captain Hiller, the pilot, know about that feature? And since they've been sitting there visible for a good 10 seconds, why haven't the aliens seen them yet?

-The aliens figure out that Area 51 exists. Connie's worried, but gung-ho Major Mitchell brushes her off. "This facility is buried deep within the mountain, that should provide us with some protection." Really? Tell that to the folks at NORAD...

-This may not be a nit--maybe the aliens just aren't that efficient. But comparing the big alien ship with a U.S. ship, like an aircraft carrier, there's tons of empty, apparently unused space. Kinda weird, if you think about it.

-As the aliens start blasting away at Area 51, a couple more of those dangerous jeeps explode.

-Some of these nits I only picked up on the latest viewing, but this one bothered me way back on August 18th, 1996: the base is under attack, everybody's panicking to get to a place of safety and they all climb into an <u>elevator</u>?? Does Area 51 not have stairs?

-The MISSILE LOCKED screen in the airplanes has a four-digit number on it that doesn't seem to correspond to anything whatsoever.

-Good old Russell. He identifies himself to the President and fires off a snappy salute...not realizing, apparently, that he's on a radio.

-These alien fellers aren't <u>that</u> smart... They've come to destroy all humans and take over the Earth, and they're getting ready for invasion when unexpectedly a scout ship from 30 years earlier shows up. It somehow got within range of the Mother ship's autopilot on its own, though there appear to be no occupants. There is a new, large, unexplained device hanging from the underside. Then suddenly after this ship shows up, a mysterious and debilitating virus infects the Mother ship. All this time, the alien in the control tower just stares at the ship, doing nothing whatsoever. He doesn't call for any investigation, he doesn't shut the ship down (and he's got control over the ship systems, he proves this by opening the blast shield)...he does nothing.

-It's also interesting that the technology and design of the alien ships hasn't changed significantly in 40 years. (I guess when you find a design that works...)

-During the big battle, the President fires his number one missile <u>twice</u>. The President's missile fails and Eagle 2 storms in, "I'm on it!"--except the exterior shot of his plane shows <u>he</u> doesn't have any missiles either.

-Luckily, one strike into the heart of this enormous craft sets off a chain reaction that destroys the whole thing. (The Death Star effect.) Also, it's rather fortunate for everybody that the alien ship, which was hovering, unmoving, directly over Area 51, chose to crash a few miles away, and not right on top of everyone...

-The General says "Get everyone on the horn"--by which he means the Morse Code machines--"and tell them how to take the sons of bitches down." Okay, so first you have to present an attractive target, get the ship to hover directly over it, then send a kamikaze pilot up into the green beam of death right before the ship fires. Well, that's simple enough...

-When David and Captain Hiller fly to the alien mother ship, get trapped and set off their nuclear bomb, David's keyboard strokes don't match what appears on-screen.

-It sure was nice of the military to put an external timer on that big nuclear missile David and Steve shoot into the Mother ship's innards. I don't know <u>why</u> they did, but it was nice of them to let us know how much time was left.

-More evidence that the aliens aren't that bright--David and Steve just barely make it out before the big doors close, the shot cuts back inside, and we see the alien ships explode as they smash into those same doors. Not one of them had the sense to apply the brakes.

-That's America for you--<u>we</u> figured out the virus, <u>we</u> figured out how to take the enemy ships down...we <u>rock</u>!

-The nuclear blast is so huge, so impressive, that we can actually <u>hear</u> it, despite the so-often-forgotten fact that THERE'S NO SOUND...oh, never mind.

-The two jeeps approach the crash site, and stop a few hundred yards away. They couldn't come a <u>little</u> closer? "Make these guys walk to us, they look like they need some exercise."

-Where did David's dad come from? President's talking to David, and he turns away, empty background all the way to the mountains, and then suddenly Julian is standing there. (The aliens brought him back!)

-Everybody seems so happy and excited that the aliens are defeated...of course, most of the world's population is dead, the economic, political and social infrastructure has been almost completely destroyed and that's nuclear fallout falling through Earth's atmosphere...kind of a Pyrrhic victory, really.

#26:   Spider-Man

Ruminations: Honestly, the one thing I really want to get off my chest is a rant about the fershlugginer webs coming out of Peter's <u>wrists!</u> I know the decision was made because it would seem implausible that a high-school kid could invent a super-adhesive, but the web-shooters were <u>cool</u>, as well as a convenient plot device. Whenever the writers needed Pete to be in a little bit more trouble, they could always have him run out of web fluid. The web-out-of-his-wrists deal along with the little spider spines coming out of his fingers <u>really</u> bugs me. (Perhaps the worst thing about it all is that now, in the comics, Peter's webbing has suddenly for no good reason gone internal, just to match the movies. Aaaarghhh!)

0:06:30-Well, let's get the <u>Will Award</u> out of the way right off the bat. As much as I like my comic-book superheroes, I still find it very lucky that the irradiated spider gave Peter Parker special abilities...and not some horrible debilitating cancerous disease.

0:06:40-Peter's lip-sync seems off as he expounds about the electron microscope.

0:08:53-When Mary Jane says "There's only fourteen," referring to the spiders, the position of her arm changes between shots.

0:09:00-So this incredibly valuable super spider escapes, and some high-school kid is the first to notice? That doesn't seem right.

0:10:30-How come Pete gets some spider abilities and not others? He doesn't, for example, grow an extra four arms, nor an extra 6 eyes. And furthermore, why do the webs come out of his wrists? (I mean, let's consider where the webs come out of an actual spider...that would sure make for some interesting visuals!)

0:10:45-Good thing for us that when Peter gets bitten, he doesn't say a word about it to anyone. Otherwise they'd have taken him to the hospital and done everything possible to un-irradiate his blood. Which would make a much less interesting movie.

0:11:31-Osborn reports that the primary test went almost completely perfectly, only one rat showed levels of insanity. Just curious, but how exactly do you measure "insanity" levels in a rat? (Or any other creature?)

0:12:50-Just a note: Uncle Ben is sixty-eight years old, and he's checking the want ads for a job. Kids, save for retirement!!

0:13:50-Dumb teenager. Peter's been bitten by an irradiated spider, the bite is swelling up something fierce and he feels awful...and he says nothing to his aunt and uncle, even though he needs serious medical attention. Oh well, it turns out all right.

0:14:00-As much as Aunt May and Uncle Ben care about Peter, and given the way he came home, I'm surprised they didn't check on him at least once...and if they <u>did</u>, why didn't they call for an ambulance?

0:14:45-We see an effect montage of the super-spider DNA replacing sections of Peter's DNA code. Assuming his DNA was already complete, what did he <u>lose</u> in this transformation? ("Gee, I sure miss my sense of smell...)

0:15:29-Is the lab-coat-wearing-guy working with Osborn just there for show? Norman asks for a specific chemical, and lab-coat has to ask him what it's for. Does that seem right?

0:15:45-Why does Norman break the bottle after he drinks it?

0:16:00-This momentous, world-changing laboratory event is happening and they're not making any sort of recording of the events? (Which is lucky, because Norman has to get away with murder...)

0:16:00-As they work in the laboratory, both Norman and lab-coat change positions between shots several times.

0:17:00-Isn't the point of head restraints to make it impossible to move one's head? Norman has several inches of travel--and it looks like he hurts himself!

0:17:25-After Norman changes himself, right before he kills his associate, there's a green reflection in lab-coat's glasses that isn't represented by his point-of-view shot.

0:17:30-If the Oscorp people are telling the truth, only one of the clinical trials had an aberration, and that was just <u>one</u> subject. What a bummer that the first human trial goes so terribly wrong. I mean hey, the odds were with Norman!

0:17:30-The green gas filling the chamber sure dissipates quickly, doesn't it?

0:17:45-So Norman Osborn injects himself with the gas, goes crazy, kills his lab assistant, and somehow gets himself home with the flight suit and glider <u>and</u> a snazzy Green Goblin mask (which he got <u>where</u>?) and <u>nobody</u> witnesses his escape.

0:18:00-Does it make sense that the spider bite fixes Pete's myopia? (And does anybody know where I can find an irradiated spider? I'm tired of wearing glasses!)

0:20:05-The morning after the bite, Peter is out on the street trying to come to grips with everything. The school bus turns the corner, then a convertible pulls in out of nowhere. When we see the bus again ten seconds later, it hasn't moved, and it freezes again when the convertible pulls out.

0:22:07-As Mary Jane falls, throwing her food up in the air, the bowl of jello and the sandwich go sideways, yet somehow still land right-side up.

0:24:50-From being in a fight at all, much less the force with which Peter hits Flash, I'm pretty sure the police would be called. There's certainly enough witnesses.

0:25:53-Okay, we have to accept that the super-sticking ability is not because he can just <u>stick</u>, but because these black spines grow out of his skin. And somehow those same spines work perfectly well on <u>metal, plastic, stone, anything</u>. All right, I'll let that pass. However, as Peter climbs his first wall, he does so with <u>shoes on</u>! Are the spines poking all the way out through the leather?

0:25:57-Besides the shoes, the shot of Peter climbing his first wall just doesn't work--he's not constricting his muscles as if he were pulling himself up, he's just moving forward. (As if he was somehow on a flat surface...)

0:27:45-Peter's rooftop jump is fairly obviously CG. He also changes position between shots as he swings.

0:27:45-It's rather a dumb experiment for Peter to test out his webbing for the first time by swinging on it. He has no idea how strong it is, or how adhesive. Then Peter seems surprised that his first web-swing leads to him slamming into the wall on the other side. Did super-smart Peter Parker forget his physics classes?

0:27:45-As Peter tests his webbing by swinging across the street, shrieking like a little girl, not <u>one</u> person looks up. Are New Yorkers <u>that</u> blasé?

0:28:15-Does it seem right that steady, responsible Uncle Ben and Aunt May would leave dirty paint supplies sitting all over the place?

0:31:10-As Peter and M.J. talk in the backyard, her hair changes between shots.

0:32:32-Peter is always short of funds--he should hire himself out as a comic-book artist! Look at the drawings he makes as he designs his spider costume...they look like the work of a professional!

0:33:17-Why does Peter's webbing break the glass on the family picture?

0:33:40-Peter passes off the weird noises coming from his room as "exercising." I refuse to believe Aunt May can't see the webbing all over the place, even though the door is only open a crack. (She's old, perhaps her eyesight isn't so great.)

0:33:55-Freeze-frame the close-up newspaper shots in this movie. Two reasons why: the filmmakers went to the trouble of writing actual stories instead of filling the lines with gobbledygook...and there are also some mistakes. I couldn't find anything wrong with "Is This the End of Norman Osborn?" but others later have problems...

0:34:45-Uncle Ben and Peter have a heart-to-heart outside the library, and Uncle Ben makes the famous "With great power comes great responsibility" speech. What great power is he talking about? He knows nothing of what's happened to Peter.

0:35:22-As Uncle Ben and Peter have their little talk, the cars passing behind them appear and disappear as the shot changes. Also, Ben's lips seem off sync at times.

0:36:30-More vanishing cars. As Peter gets out of Ben's car and Ben drives away, in the time that we look away from Peter and back again, the sedan and bicyclist that were coming up behind him have been replaced by a police car. Poof!

0:36:40-This wrestling deal...it's like an Ultimate Fighting Championship combined with the World Wrestling Federation. On one hand, you've got stupid costumes and theatrics, and anybody with a costume can get into the ring, yet on the other hand it appears to be real fighting. Seems like this sort of thing would give New York a bad name...

0:36:40-It's weird that we can't hear the noise from the arena until Pete gets up the stairs and there's an accompanying visual.

0:36:55-During the first wrestling match, the wrestlers change positions as the shot changes. The one that gets thrown out of the ring is obviously on wires.

0:39:14-The lovely, genteel ladies that encourage Peter as he walks towards the ring have some lip-syncing problems.

0:39:40-The arena management certainly can't expect this little kid to last long against Bonesaw, yet they put the cage bars down for some reason. Why waste a cage match on such an obviously outmatched fight? (Of course, without the cage, Spidey couldn't show off his abilities...)

0:41:40-Further proof that the arena managers aren't that bright--this punk kid just took out an opponent twice his size in a matter of seconds...but instead of giving Peter a contract, they stiff him!

0:42:40-The arena cop to Peter: "What the hell's the matter with you, you let him go!" I still remember the training program at <u>Arby's</u> (stop laughing, everybody has a first job) telling me that if somebody demanded the money in the counter...<u>give it to him</u>. Be polite about it. No amount of money is worth a person's life. So I find the cop's attitude unseemly.

0:42:43-During the arena robbery, the manager gets hit on the forehead...but as he runs up to Peter he's holding the <u>back</u> of his head.

0:43:25-As Peter arrives at the scene of Uncle Ben's carjacking, the people behind him change positions with the changing shot several times. Peter also pushes his way into the crowd twice. The lady officer telling Peter to stay back pushes him twice.

0:44:30-CPR is an option some time after a victim stops breathing (I've heard as long as 45 minutes.) NY cops should certainly know CPR procedures, but Uncle Ben's lying on the ground and nobody's doing anything.

0:44:38-How cold is it that Peter leaves his just-deceased beloved Uncle behind to chase down the criminal?

0:50:35-As the Green Goblin shows up for his first attack, we hear him laughing from some distance. Does Gobby have an amplifier built into that spiffy mask, or does he just <u>really</u> know how to project?

0:54:58-Spider-man foils a robbery, and the two crooks are found suspended in a large, elaborate web. Real spiders build that kind of thing one strand at a time. Is that how Spidey did it? ("Hang on, I'm almost finished, then we'll stick you up here and I'll be on my way...")

0:55:09-Freeze-frame the "Masked Man" newspaper article. The text repeats itself over and over. So does "Man Climbs Wall Like Spider."

0:55:14-In the what's-Spidey-up-to montage, one of the police officers says Spider-man is "some kind of freaky-doo." At least, that's what the soundtrack says. The cops lips might be saying "fluffy-doo" or "fairy-doo" but they're <u>not</u> saying "freaky-doo."

0:55:24-Spidey averts a purse-snatching and somehow leaves a "Courtesy your friendly neighborhood Spider-man" note...despite never being within three feet of the purse. (That same purse disappears in the wide shot, then reappears)

0:55:49-If Peter can't get work as a comic-book artist, he could become a costume designer--seriously, his outfit is the most <u>amazing</u> home-made superhero costume I have <u>ever</u> seen! (And I should know, I spent a good long time working on a homemade Batman outfit when I was in junior-hi...um, let's just move on.)

0:56:34-Why is Jameson unaware that the previous day's Bugle sold out?

0:57:30-As Peter and Mary Jane talk outside the diner where she works, the people in the background appear and disappear willy-nilly.

1:00:52-A further display of heroics has Spider-man foiling an armed car robbery. The armored car is sideways, blocked in by a car accident, and the security guard gets out and opens the back. Something tells me this is <u>not</u> standard operating procedure when something out of the ordinary has your armored car blocked in.

1:01:11-Peter's camera has a very strange "random picture" setting--he's webbed it up so it can take pictures of himself saving the day, but it doesn't go off in any recognizable pattern. And later, when he shows the photos to Jameson, there's one of Spider-man in mid-air. How did Peter get that photo?

1:02:48-Perhaps I don't understand big business, but the Oscorp board seems to sell out Norman very easily. It's his company, after all. Also, Oscorp is (or should be) currently dealing with a murder investigation...is that a good time to be forcing out the company's founder? Wouldn't that look a little suspicious?

1:04:18-Just a note in passing: the festival has some really ugly floats.

1:04:36-During the festival song, Macy Gray changes positions between her first and second shot.

1:05:35-Pete's spider-sense sure has a long range. At the festival, the Green Goblin isn't even in sight yet, and Pete reacts like something's wrong.

1:05:55-This glider is something incredible. It has enough fuel to sustain prolonged flight, along with rockets and guns and bullets...where is all this stuff stored?

1:06:30-As the Goblin makes his first turn there's a strange boom--he's certainly not breaking the sound barrier, and nothing explodes...did the glider backfire?

1:06:40-Osborn sure has been busy. He gets a fancy mask someplace, he makes all these different types of bombs that go along with his Goblin motif...

1:06:45-Green Goblin has a pumpkin bomb that just explodes, a pumpkin bomb that releases metal blades, and a pumpkin bomb that vaporizes, which he uses to turn the board members into ashy skeletons. The bombs look exactly the same. I think this could lead to problems. Plus, how does Osborn know how to fly the glider? And is it bright for him to shout "Out, am I?" in front of witnesses before committing murder?

1:06:45-Gobby's pumpkin bomb hits on the stone face of the building, yet windows up to thirty feet away blow out. This seems a bit much.

1:06:45-This is an interesting one: freeze-frame right after the bomb hits the balcony. There's a shot of the crowd and only Peter is looking up at the balcony...that is, only Peter and this chick right in front of him. She's also looking up at the balcony, and for some reason she's grinning. (Seems like a "Hey mom, I got my face in the movie!" kind of smile.)

1:06:47-Between that wide shot of the crowd and the close-up of Peter, the people behind him suddenly change position.

1:06:55-Did everybody catch Spider-man creator Stan Lee's cameo in the crowd shot? Just checking...

1:07:03-Peter saves a couple from falling stone--they're facing towards him, running, and a half-second later when we come back to them they've turned around, switched positions, and are now just watching the stone fall.

1:07:13-Is it Spider-man's day off? This is Mr. "With great power comes great responsibility", Peter the-whole-world-is-relying-on-me-to-save-them Parker. His spider sense warns him about the Goblin's approach, the first explosions go off...and thirty seconds later he's finally getting into costume. What's the holdup?

1:07:15-The shot as Peter rips open his shirt to reveal his costume is a direct homage to the first Superman movie.

1:07:33-Lucky that the skeletonizing pumpkin bomb only vaporized in one direction--Harry and M.J. sure seem to be in range on the other side.

1:07:56-The glider must be thought-controlled, or have very tiny controls in the little foot-holders, because Gobby keeps firing off rockets and bullets without touching anything. Later we see him control the glider with buttons on the back of his left wrist--but he's not touching those buttons in this scene. (I also don't know <u>where</u> he keeps pulling those pumpkin bombs from.)

1:08:05-Spider-man sees a kid about to be squashed by a falling float. He swings down from the balcony to save him. He's pointed pretty much upright in one shot, but when he gets to the kid he's suddenly sideways.

1:08:22-Gobby knows that you've got to diversify, you can't just rely on one talent--so he's practicing his ventriloquism. And he's very good: after Spider-man saves the kid, we see a very close close-up of Gobby, who says "Impressive" without moving his mouth one little bit.

1:08:25-As the Goblin throws Spider-man and our hero crashes through roughly thirty-seven things, his position changes during the lengthy process.

1:09:36-I called my teacher/engineer/all-around smart guy friend Dave Boom to crunch the numbers on this one. Earlier a piece of the balcony broke off, and it took five seconds to hit the ground, which put the balcony around <u>400 feet</u> in the air. (Which is much higher than it really is.) Here, when Mary Jane falls, it takes her <u>eight</u> seconds to almost hit the ground, which means she fell from <u>over a thousand feet up</u>.

1:09:40-You can tell it's a stuntwoman falling, and not Kirsten Dunst.

1:10:07-It's supposedly so romantic that after Spider-man saves Mary Jane from certain death he swings away with her across the city. I can only speak for myself, but between the near-death trauma and the motion sickness, I would not find this experience very romantic.

1:10:09-Screw the laws of physics: somehow as Spider-man finished his cross-town swing with Mary Jane, he makes a turn on his webbing and also slows down.

1:13:03-Quick note: Willem Dafoe puts in a great performance as a crazed supervillain. Especially the scene where he's talking to himself in the mirror. Fantastic!

1:13:23-How good is this personality-switching ability? We see more than once that Osborn is switching from good to evil literally, not just figuratively. (He changes expressions as we watch.) Later, he goes back and forth between one frame and the next as the shot changes. That is seriously fast psyche switching!

1:13:29-More newspaper follies: "Oscorp Board Murdered" mentions the Green Goblin's glider as a rocket-powered skateboard device, the word riding is misspelled ridding, there are missing commas, the text repeats itself halfway through, and finally the article has no byline. On second thought, given the mistakes, that last might have been on purpose.

1:14:18-Jameson holds up a Daily Bugle with a picture of Spider-man and the Goblin duking it out. The picture must have been taken from the balcony...so who took the picture? Mary Jane?

1:14:26-When Jameson calls Hoffman on the phone, his head turns twice.

1:15:00-Peter seems as surprised as anyone when the Green Goblin smashes in. Where did his long-range spider-sense go?

1:18:00-Peter and Mary Jane have another street-side conversation where people and cars appear and disappear throughout.

1:18:18-Mary Jane: "They said I needed acting lessons." I'll bet Kirsten Dunst just loved that line. It's the sort of thing that will be played back during interviews for the rest of her career.

1:20:02-When Peter saves Mary Jane from the would-be muggers, M.J.'s position changes as the shot changes when the muggers are ripped away.

1:20:08-How do the muggers pull the webbing off themselves that fast? This stuff is strong enough and adhesive enough to pull the side of a building off.

1:21:07-When this movie came out, everybody made a big deal about the upside-down kiss. What's so special and romantic about water running up your nose? Tobey Maguire admits he almost choked during those takes. Come to think of it, it kinda makes M.J. look like a tramp. Yes, Spider-man just saved her virtue, but she doesn't know that it's Peter, so basically she's making out with a complete stranger.

1:21:43-Between frames Peter gets his mask back into position.

1:21:45-After the kiss, Spidey disappears straight upwards. Even if Peter is somehow pulling his webs back into his body, I don't know how he can rise straight up that fast.

1:22:20-Cut to a burning tenement, and the child trapped inside. (There's always a child trapped inside. Why is that?) A woman on the street shouts, "Look up there!" She must have really amazing eyesight, because we cut to where Spidey is swinging through the city--and he looks to be about a mile from the burning house.

1:24:18-Lucky for Peter that all of Green Goblin's bombs look alike--so that Gobby used his spinning-blade bomb instead of the skeletonizer. Spidey would have had a hard time avoiding that.

1:24:50-As Gobby and Spidey fight in the burning building, Spider-man's kick is shown twice.

1:25:08-The New York police department--at least in the Marvel comics universe--doesn't seem to be too bright. Somebody murdered an Oscorp lab assistant, somebody also murdered most of the Oscorp board, shouting "Out, am I?" as he did so...and Norman Osborn, the founder of Oscorp, isn't in custody as a prime suspect? No...he's attending Thanksgiving dinner with the Parkers!

1:26:11-Osborn can sure move quietly. Aunt May suspects Peter is upstairs, and you hear her going up the stairs. There's no sound of anyone following her, yet when she turns the corner Osborn is right behind.

1:26:15-Osborn pushes into Peter's room during Thanksgiving dinner. This trick is used a lot in martial-arts and superhero movies--the one where somebody is hiding right above somebody else, and the person below has no idea the other person is there. Is it really possible to miss somebody that close?

1:26:38-Osborn turns away, and stops as a drop of blood hits the floor. He couldn't hear Peter breathing right above him, or any sound when Peter flung himself out the window, but he hears a drop of blood hit the floor. And, suddenly, because there's a drop of blood on the floor and Pete has a cut on his arm, Osborn realizes that out of the eight-or-so million people in New York, Peter Parker is Spider-man.

1:27:15-Safely undiscovered, Peter grabs his street clothes, swings away, changes, stops to buy some cranberry sauce...but forgets to bandage his bleeding wound. Whoops...

1:31:31-Parker makes a logic-jump of his own: Aunt May describes the "horrible yellow eyes" of her attacker, and somehow Peter immediately knows that it's the Green Goblin. He doesn't know Gobby has figured out his secret, and there are surely other animals or creatures in New York with yellow eyes...

1:31:46-There's a photo of the Parker family next to Aunt May's bed. Did Peter go home, get the photo and bring it back, or did the paramedics grab that when they left for the hospital?

1:39:35-Peter Parker's best-friend's father becomes Spider-man's very first archenemy. What are the odds??

1:40:45-Both Spider-man and the Green Goblin are incredibly strong. During the bridge scene, both support the entire weight of a cable car full of cub scouts. Do you have any idea how heavy that must be?

1:42:20-Gobby forces Spidey to choose between saving the kids or saving Mary Jane. Considering how little time he has to do either, it seems odd that he would stand there and think about it for ten seconds after Gobby lets go.

1:42:40-Where does the rest of the cable go? Green Goblin cuts one side, then suddenly a few shots later there's just a short piece left, somehow attached to the roof of the cable car. Whaaaaa?

1:44:43-Thank goodness the cable suddenly gets long enough that Spider-man has enough slack to lower the car to the waiting barge. When Spidey catches the car, the cable only looks about a third that long.

1:45:00-When the Goblin throws Spider-man into the abandoned building, after Spidey saves Mary Jane and the cub scouts, the cable he's still holding onto suddenly disappears.

1:45:15-Spider-man lucks out--again--that Gobby doesn't use one of those skeletonize bombs, just one that blows him around a bit.

1:46:08-As Gobby and Spidey fight their last battle, Spider-man creates a web that the Green Goblin tears apart with a bending-iron-type sound. Is Spidey's webbing made of metal?

1:46:55-Gobby threatens Spidey with his fancy trident (which came from where, exactly?) and Spidey gets mad and throws Gobby...and at that point the trident disappears.

1:47:43-Spider-man hits the Goblin...and again there's a metallic sound. I'll buy that Gobby's mask is metal, but is Spidey's fist?

1:48:51-As Norman Osborn begs for his life, there's a beautiful lighting effect on his face...and where is this lighting coming from?

1:49:13-Osborn changes position between frames right as the glider hits him. His hands move, his expression changes, and suddenly he's a foot or so away from the wall.

1:49:14-Considering that the glider blades just drove through an entire person, there's remarkably little blood on them. It's also kind-of lucky for Osborn that he dies quick. That wound would be remarkably painful, I figure.

1:49:30-Lucky that during that whole battle royale, Peter didn't take any blows to the face--those would be hard to explain at Norman Osborn's funeral.

1:54:00-After M.J. and Peter kiss, as he says "I want you to know that I will always be there for you," her hand jumps around Peter's face between frames.

1:55:20-Spidey's closing web montage flies right in the face of physics. He's swinging down the middle of the street...what is he attached to? In the middle of one swing he suddenly rises hundreds of feet in the air. At the end he's swinging right at the camera even though the web is stretched off to one side...

2:00:31-Quick note about the closing credits: you can't even mention Albert Einstein's name without giving somebody credit? All Aunt May said was something about Einstein's room being messy. It's not like they expounded at length about his Theory of Relativity. "Albert Einstein courtesy Roger Richman Agency, Inc." Sheesh... (Albert Einstein courtesy Roger Richman Agency, Inc.)

#27:   Star Wars IV: A New Hope

Ruminations: My Empire Strikes Back review mentioned T.A. Chapin & Polly Luttrell, true Star Wars nerds and nitpickers extraordinaire. Between themselves, in the preview to their book, they claim to have seen the SW movies, like, 800 times.

So how'd I find 50 nits they missed, I ask you?

8-)

-02:14   Opening shot is an absolute cinematic marvel, that I would not dare nitpick. (Though for the record, the vacuum of space sure is loud around here!)

-03:05   A moment ago Threepio's head was very shiny—now it's really dusty

-07:15   "The damage doesn't look as bad from out here." Does Threepio have some sort of binocular vision?

They're 10, 15 miles away from the ship and falling fast—how can he tell how bad the damage looks?

-07:42   Continuity, stormtroopers behind Leia

-09:20   How'd they land this falling pad in what looks like 30 feet of disturbed sand? (And is that big blue thing off the side of the pod their parachute? Suppose it could be, but it looks weird)

-10:20   Does it make <u>any</u> sense for the robots to split up? Or have an <u>argument</u> about splitting up?

-11:51   How does R2 even move in this environment?

-12:04   Ha! I nitpicked while listening to the DVD commentary. At this point Lucas is talking, and he describes the vehicle Luke is riding in as a "sandspeeder." Now I'm a bit of a Star Wars geek, and I've heard of sandcrawlers, and landspeeders (which is what Luke is in right now) but never a <u>sandspeeder</u>...

-12:50   Continuity as Jawas lift Artoo

-13:50   The Jawas want to sell our little blue robot pal. He needs to be in as good shape as possible. So they <u>suck</u> him haphazardly into the crawler?

-15:37   "Look sir, droids!" Stormtrooper's got <u>one</u> little piece of metal...is there a manufacture stamp on it? How can that one little circle prove droids have been here in this very un-droidlike environment?

-16:02   I don't know if this is a nit or not, but it's my book. Artoo has several lights around his dome. There's a round one that goes from blue to red, and a couple longer rectangulary lights that have always, far as I can tell, been blue. Thing is, in a coupla shots one or more of these lights are <u>green</u>, and it seems wrong. In addition to the above time, look also at 16:12, 16:17, 16:29

-19:40   Luke saunters down the steps into the shop, followed by the droids. How, exactly, is R2 supposed to get down here? (Oh yeah, he has those jets in his legs, doesn't he?)

-19:46   If you've seen the prequel, A—you have my pity, and 2—you know that somebody thought it would make sense for little Anakin Skywalker to have <u>built</u> Threepio in his little slave hut. (Yeah, don't get me started.) So it seems odd that Threepio, coming back to the planet of his birth, has nothing to say about such. (There's talk of Threepio having had his memory erased in his adventure-laden past, but I think the whole thing is just stupid so I mention it.)

-19:55   Artoo has that green light again

-20:10   I would think Threepio's exposed wiring wouldn't be a good thing to dip in lubricant

-21:35   "Who is that? She's <u>beautiful</u>." Luke has fallen hard for this 6-inch hologram...kid <u>really</u> needs to get off this planet

-21:40   Is Threepio just dissembling? He is a protocol droid, despite no other evidence of protocol throughout his film career. He says here that he has no idea who Princess Leia is—which seems odd considering her importance.

-23:00   "Play back the whole message." R2 claims he has no message to play. So...the droids aren't First Law safe, being as they can <u>lie</u> to humans

-23:07   Minor continuity from Threepio as Aunt Beru calls to Luke

-23:20   Right here as Threepio and Artoo have a chat, when we cut to the close-up of R2, we should see 3PO's arm, he's close enough. But we don't. Also 23:25, 23:28.

By the way, I just noticed that I'm referring to robots as "he" instead of "it." I'm going to continue to do so because the other way is weird

-24:19　Continuity. Luke starts to pull the glass away from his mouth, then next frame he's still drinking!

-25:15　Luke storms out of the dining room, and we cut to Aunt Beru. Three seconds later back to Uncle Owen, and Luke is all the way across the courtyard. Did the kid break into a sprint when we weren't looking, then slow to a walk right when we do? Why would he do that?

-25:36　I have it on good authority that any planet under the light of twin suns would <u>not</u> be able to sustain life

-25:50　And these suns are weird, too. Between the last time we saw them and this shot, they've moved <u>much</u> closer together! In ten seconds!

-26:46　Do the fancy graphics in Luke's macrobinoculars correspond to anything? They don't seem to

-27:51　Luke and Threepio are out looking for their missing droid friend. Luke says, and I quote: "Hit the accelerator!" Um...seriously? Threepio is <u>driving</u>?

-28:00　Sand Person (well, they're Sand People, aren't they? Anyway) has a bead on the landspeeder, when his friend pulls him away. Why didn't the guy fire? How much fresh, unaware meat can drive by on Tatooine?

-28:05　Wanna know how they made that cool Bantha? The ones that aren't computer generated? They got some poor circus elephant and put <u>that</u> getup on him and made him stand around in the Tunisian sun. Shame on Lucas and all of his 1977 cronies

-28:30　How did Artoo get so far out here? Those jets we never saw in the classic movies?

-29:00　Continuity on Sand Person

-29:03   Famous one: Sand Person's reaction shot as he towers over Luke is reversed near the end, because the editor didn't have a long enough clip

-29:18   Why did they park the landspeeder on a rock? (Because it was easier to do that than simulate the hover, of course)

-29:26   Continuity, Sand People around landspeeder

-30:08   Wow. Life on Tatooine must be very hard. Granted, 20 years ago Obi-Wan went through some difficult circumstances, but still—he looks to have aged about 40 years!

-32:10   All Threepio did was fall backwards...yet his entire <u>arm</u> came off? I suppose Anakin didn't do all that great a job building him...

-32:30   And now the <u>robot</u> is having a pity party. How (and for that matter <u>why</u>) do these creations have the ability to feel emotion?

-32:55   "I was once a Jedi Knight, same as your father." After Kenobi's statement, Luke now knows that his father was a Jedi. Weren't Jedi a big deal? It's like being told your previously unknown father had been a master Samurai, or world leader...yet Luke has no appreciable reaction to the revelation

-33:07   "I hear you're quite a good pilot yourself." It's Tatooine, and Luke is a whiny teenager. What in the <u>world</u> has he been flying? Don't tell me the landspeeder counts! I know, prior to this conversation he used to "bulls-eye w] womprats" in his "T-16", but still...

-33:10   Kenobi, speaking of Anakin: "And he was a good friend." Yeah, sure, if you leave out all those psychotic episodes

-33:44   Ben just <u>hands over</u> this incredibly important, incredibly expensive, incredibly rare, incredibly <u>dangerous</u> weapon? The one that can cut through <u>anything</u> but another lightsaber? To the excitable, easily distracted teenage kid? Lucky the old guy didn't lose an arm

-33:49   Glass rod lightsaber visible here in still frame. (Couldn't <u>believe</u> my fellow Star Wars nerds missed this one!)

-36:44   And Luke just casually waves the saber around, this blade that could cut through <u>anything</u> in the room…

-40:40   Wow, are those bodies charred. This still a PG movie?

-42:45   "You'll never find a more wretched hive of scum and villainy." Is Obi-Wan just grumpy? Mos Eisley's no Alderaan, but it doesn't seem to be <u>that</u> bad

-43:35   Is Kenobi's Jedi mind-trick affecting all the troopers? If not, does it make sense for the five guys <u>not</u> being affected not to say anything? "Hey, Gary—you know that guy just used a Jedi whammy on you, right?"

-46:45   "You better watch yourself. I have the death sentence on twelve systems." What does that second sentence even mean?

-48:07   "It's the ship that made the Kessel run in less than twelve parsecs." Oh, sure, Lucas goes to great length on the commentary to explain that this <u>isn't</u> a mistake. But it is. Sorry, George. A parsec is a measure of length, not time.

-54:33   Poor Artoo, left behind to try and scramble down a set of steps…

-56:38   "Traveling through hyperspace ain't like dusting crops, boy!" This is a long time ago in a far, far away galaxy. Yet they still say "dusting crops?"

-57:10   Princess Leia shown post interrogation. That droid sure looked ominous, but it must not have done much, because she doesn't look at all shaken or disturbed...even the cinnamon buns are still in place!

-58:57   Ha! The Death Star weapons panel...find a television station old enough (I used to work at one) and you'll see the <u>exact</u> same panel in the production studio! The Death Star Laser is run by a Grass Valley switcher!

-59:03   I mention this in my <u>Return of the Jedi</u> review, also—what's the worst job in the Empire? Being one of the guys standing in the laser trench! What are these guys supposed to do, besides absorb a whole bunch of radiation?

-59:30   Right here Kenobi hears "millions of voices crying out in terror, then suddenly silenced" or suchlike. Did the whole planet of Alderaan only have a few million people on it, or were only a few million aware enough of their doom to cry out? And how, when the Death Star superlaser explosion happened pretty much instantly? While I'm on the subject, how does that instant destruction work, anyway? Do planets all have dynamite at their core?

-1:01:04 Now Luke is practicing his saber tricks in the <u>Falcon</u>'s romper room. Sure seems like a very small space for lightsaber practice

-1:01:11 Jump cut as Luke douses the saber. I want to go easy on this one because they didn't have fancy computers to do all their dirty work back then, so Mark Hamill had to try and hold perfectly still while some production assistant plucked the "extended" lightsaber out of his hand and replaced it with the "doused" version. But you can still see the cut—and since this is the remastered, whoop-de-do digital version of the film, I'm surprised it's not fixed!

-1:01:50 Is there a point to having the ability to make one's helmet completely opaque? Just for those times when you <u>know</u> a blast is imminent, I suppose...

-1:01:52 Jump cut, as Luke relights his saber. And why isn't it green?

-1:01:58 Now the teenage kid with the dangerous weapon is <u>blind</u>, in the previously mentioned small space

-1:09:00 What are the odds—the two stormtroopers that walk into the <u>Falcon</u> to check on things are the exact same size as Han and Luke! (And where did that scanning team go, anyway?)

-1:09:12 Artoo has that green light again

-1:11:48 "More wealth than you can imagine." As Luke says this, the subtitles on the DVD say "More well than you can imagine"

-1:12:00 Huh. Luke goes from being a whiny farm boy to being a brilliant tactician in just a few hours—he and Han are on the Death Star and Han asks <u>him</u> what the plan is for Princess Rescue?

-1:12:35 Chewie roars at a droid. Well and good, but why does this little droid act <u>scared</u>? Why would a robot be <u>programmed</u> with <u>fear</u>?

-1:12:40 Nice of the Imperials to leave Wookiee restraints lying around

-1:14:16 "Prisoner transfer from cell block 1138"—everybody catch the reference to Lucas's first film?

-1:14:58 At this moment an Imperial falls down after a nearby flash—that doesn't seem to come even close to hitting him

-1:15:10 Han's telling Luke where the Princess is. How? He's looking at a blank panel!

-1:15:40 Amazing that the Imperials let Leia keep her makeup kit with her in the cell and all. Gal looks great, despite imprisonment and torture!

-1:16:30 Moff Tarkin, on Kenobi: "Surely he must be dead by now." Why? The guy's only 50 or so, right? (wink, wink)

-1:17:10 We see a little mouse droid rolling away, just past a six-inch step. How'd he get over that?

-1:18:34 So one laser blast blew the dumpster grille off nice and neat? How? One thing's for sure, they certainly won't get the Wookiee down there

-1:20:40 "My gun's jammed!" So why are you still holding it?

-1:21:06 Continuity, Princess Leia. Back to front, as shot changes

-1:21:17 Continuity, Solo and Skywalker coming out of the water

-1:21:30 Long metal bar next to the Princess was covered a frame ago, now completely clear of debris

-1:22:05 Trash compactor continuity

-1:22:22 Luke's calling for Threepio, and when we cut to the droids, his voice is coming over commlink. Nice of him to <u>stop</u> calling <u>just</u> when the Imperials come in, eh? And why does a droid need a hand-held commlink anyway?

-1:23:39 Continuity, trash compactor—Han's hand moves on Leia (plus it looks like Harrison touches a place Carrie might not have wanted him to)

-1:23:48 Artoo has double green this time

-1:23:58 "I forgot, I turned it off." Wow, these robot designers (Anakin, right, Anakin) put in not only prissiness, and self-pity, but the ability to <u>FORGET</u> things?!? I almost want to give that the Will Award, but not yet...

-1:24:19 Artoo green light again (1:24:25 too)

-1:24:51 Continuity. Leia is hugging Han one frame, and then the next she's jumped away. Guess she remembered his inappropriate behavior

-1:25:36 Lucky Kenobi knows how to deactivate a Death Star tractor-beam, huh? Seems like really specific info to have, but anyway...

-1:25:46 Han and Luke are back in their Tatooine outfits. Where did those come from? They go back to the original room to get 'em? (Answer: no, and neither did they carry them with—it's movie magic!)

-1:27:53 Sure ain't no OSHA in space—that missing bridge seems a bit dangerous for a workplace!

-1:27:54 Continuity, Luke at the edge of the abyss

-1:28:00 Sure are lucky stormtroopers can't shoot straight

-1:29:00 The door moves up six inches—seems like the troopers behind it could go for a foot shot, or an ankle grab, but they don't

-1:29:01 Ha! Freeze it here to watch Princess Leia fire on the stormtroopers <u>with her eyes closed</u>!!! (And the Star Wars nerds missed this one too!)

-1:29:11 The swing across the chasm happens twice, when shot changes

-1:29:12 Sure is lucky Luke had rope/grappling hook with him, and said rope was <u>just</u> long enough

-1:29:36 More green light, Artoo

-1:30:08 Continuity, lightsaber, Kenobi

-1:30:21 Interesting that Vader's shiny costume doesn't have any reflections from the <u>glowing object</u> he's holding

-1:30:43 Freeze frame here to see the glass rod instead of lightsaber, also at 1:30:54. There's some goofy fight continuity as well

-1:30:51 "If you strike me down, I shall become more powerful than you can possibly imagine." Yeah, he'll be able to appear in a ghost-like form and make pithy comments. Boogity boogity boogity

-1:32:23 How <u>does</u> Kenobi pull off his disappearing act, anyway?

-1:34:04 Han sends Luke down into the quad-gun turret. Did he teach this farmboy how to work one of these things after the lightsaber practice, on their way to Alderaan?

-1:34:24 Whew! These futuristic folks sure have some dated, circa 1977 computer graphics!

-1:34:46 This is an easy one to see, and I can't imagine <u>why</u> they didn't do something to fix on the digital version. The matting of TIE fighters is obvious, a brown box around the spaceship against the black of space. Also at 1:35:10, 1:35:16, 1:35:23. I used to have <u>American Cinematographer</u> issues with pages and pages on the Star Wars re-release. Since they bothered researching how the second-unit shots in Tunisia had been filmed, and made a thousands-and-thousands-of-polygons digital <u>Millennium Falcon</u> for this digital release, I can't imagine <u>why</u> nobody did something about this.

-1:35:41 Bummer for these TIE pilots that the Empire doesn't care about them—they're obviously sent out as cannon fodder

-1:36:00 Space sure is loud

-1:37:05 "They're obviously tracking us. That's the only explanation for the ease of our escape." So...Leia is <u>certain</u> that the ship has a tracking device on board, but they go ahead to the Rebel base anyway? Han's bugging out anyway, why not land somewhere and procure another ship?

-1:38:48 Somebody should be questioning whether or not Leia is fit for command. She was imprisoned, tortured, watched her whole planet be destroyed, and while somebody mentions that they're sorry about Alderaan, she's all "Yeah, I'll grieve later." Not healthy, Leia...

-1:39:10 How does the Death Star <u>move</u>, exactly? I don't recall ever seeing a propulsion system

-1:40:35 Yes, you saw it coming. Time for the Will Award. The Rebels have to destroy the Death Star, and how could they possibly get rid of something so big? Wait—wait—turns out there's this little thermal exhaust port, leads right to the heart of the beast, and a proton torpedo in <u>there</u> will blow up <u>the whole entire space station!!!</u>

I think <u>Family Guy</u> said it best. Stewie, as Darth Vader: "Can't we put some plywood over that, or something?"

-1:41:10 "The moon with the Rebel base will be in range in thirty minutes." It's interesting that they use minutes just like we do, but beyond that—the Imperials have a chance to bring an end to the Rebels. This thirty minutes gives the Rebels a chance, feeble though it may be, to strike back.

So...what is <u>so</u> important about the planet Yavin that the Imperials don't just <u>use the giant superlaser weapon to destroy</u> it? Does the weapon have a long recharge period or something? Is it hard to get giant superlaser ammunition?

-1:42:45 Hey, who knew Skywalker was qualified to fly an X-wing? Must be really close to that T-16 he used to bulls-eye womprats in...

-1:43:36 Continuity, Luke and Doomed...er, I mean Biggs

-1:44:48 Luke sits in his cockpit, bobbing gently back and forth. Strange how the wide shot shows an unmoving X-wing

-1:45:06 When did the <u>Falcon</u> get back from the Death Star—Leia is still running around in a dirty robe? This Princess is really focused!

-1:45:31 "All craft, report in." Now, if I wanted to hear from all of my pilots, I think I would want some sort of order. Numerical order, maybe. Not that kooky Rebellion. We get reports from Red 10, 7, 3, 6, 9, 2, 11 and 5, in that order. And how did latecomer Skywalker get assigned number 5? How did he rank above other, actual seasoned pilots? (Maybe they all gather in the hanger, and "ready set go!" run to their ships--and get numbered off based on who is the fastest)

-1:45:50 "Shields up, double front!" The pilots have to be <u>told</u> to put shields up?

-1:46:43 Red 5 dives, lasers zapping. What's he firing at? Nothing in front of him

-1:47:23 "I got a problem here." "Eject!" Eject? Does that work in space?

-1:48:28 Luke fires at an Imperial as they speed over the Death Star. Cut to a shot of a TIE fighter exploding in deep space, no Death Star anywhere around

-1:48:54 Strange X-wing design, that this very important astromech droid is so vulnerable and out in the open

-1:51:18 Back when the Death Star was "30 minutes" away from Yavin's moon, the accompanying Imperial screen said "00:30:00." Which makes quite a bit of sense. Now, however, the Imperials are "13 minutes and closing" and the screen says 00:15:12. This some new Empire math?

-1:51:35 "Luke, take Red 2 and 3..." I guess if it makes sense for Luke to be out here at all, it makes sense for him to get a battlefield promotion over more qualified guys to field commander. And why doesn't Red Leader call him Red 5 anyway?

-1:53:00 Did Vader get his billowy cape into that tiny TIE fighter cockpit?

-1:53:10 "I just lost my starboard engine!" Could you be a little more specific, sir? There are two engines on your starboard side...and why do they have the term "starboard" in this galaxy far, far away?

-1:53:26 "One minute and closing." Last time we heard anything they said "three minutes" and that was about two minutes ago, so well done. However, the graphic accompanying "One minute and closing" says 00:09:18! (Cannot BELIEVE the nerds missed this one!!!)

-1:54:05 More cockpit bounce from the X-wing closeup. Is Luke sitting on a waterbed?

-1:55:12 "Thirty seconds and closing." It took two minutes for that thirty seconds to pass!

-1:56:17 "The Death Star has cleared the planet." About time—should have happened 2:15 before now

-1:56:47 And suddenly Solo, in the Falcon, is providing the cover fire that the Rebels should have been offering each other this whole time

-1:57:08 The Death Star cleared the planet almost a minute ago, the Imperials know the Rebels are attacking— they sure are hesitant about using that giant superweapon!

-1:57:26 More with the rocking-chair X-wing cockpit

-1:57:36 How in the galaxy does Vader survive, out on his own in deep space in a short-range fighter?

-1:58:56 In the final medal scene, there are dozens of guys in flight suits. If there weren't enough spacecraft to go around for these guys to fly, how come Luke went up? Or are these just random guys dressed in flight uniforms?

-2:00:09 Look at the stars during credits—on the left side of the screen, there's a cross formation which is pretty cool

#28:   **Harry Potter and the Prisoner of Azkaban**

Ruminations: that whole PG rating thing sure ain't what it used to be...

-0:01:35 Poor Harry, back again at the Dursleys. He wants to read his book under the covers, so he loudly has to say "Lumos Maxima"—which brings his hypersensitive uncle out to see what's up. Um...there some reason the kid just can't use a flashlight under his covers, like everybody else?

-0:03:20 Hard to tell for sure, but Harry's famous scar seems absent

-0:04:00 Angry Harry, without doing a specific spell, makes lights flicker and glass break. He's been angry plenty at Hogwarts, and this has never happened...why here and now?

-0:04:42 Expanding Marge's buttons pop off—why does the one that hits the cuckoo clock makes the bird come out?

-0:05:00 Considering how bloated Marge has become, I consider all the theatergoers <u>very</u> lucky that her clothes have expanded with instead of coming off. And I'm also amazed that she still has the power of speech!

-0:05:48 When Dursley finally lets Margo go and drops to the ground, he hits twice

-0:08:18 Big black dog barks at Harry. We learn much later that this was Sirius (it may not be in the movie, but it's in the book.) Why the barking?

-0:08:25 Lucky the Night Bus was <u>right there</u> for Harry, huh?

-0:12:00 Night Bus bumps a car and the alarm goes off—so it's tangible. So it's pretty lucky that there's always <u>just</u> enough space to weave through traffic

-0:12:42 Nice touch—guy in Leaky Cauldron reading Stephen Hawking's "A Brief History of Time"

-0:14:30 Funny how Dursley related accidents always seem to fall right before the start of Hogwarts term

-0:15:25 One would think the Monster Book of Monsters would come with a warning—seems like a dangerous item!

-0:17:00 Lot of growth for our heroes between the two movies!

-0:18:35 Does it make sense to have a private conversation near pictures that can hear you, and talk amongst themselves?

-0:19:40 Sure, there's some strange guy in the same train car—let's loudly whisper secrets anyway, because he's probably asleep...

-0:20:10 The train comes to an emergency stop, yet the bottle on the end-table doesn't move. Is it glued down?

-0:21:35 These dementors sure seem scarier than a PG rating to me

-0:22:00 Read the book—the "soul kiss" of a Dementor is a last-resort for someone they have to absolutely destroy. Why in the world do they start administering such to Harry, on the Hogwarts train??

-0:24:20 Where did this Hogwarts Glee Club come from? And could they have picked a more inappropriate song? "Something wicked this way comes," honestly!

-0:24:40 Dumbledore changed form over the summer! He looks like a completely different person!

-0:26:30 "I must warn you," Dumbledore about the Dementors, "give them no reason to harm you." He doesn't explain what he means, or what harm he's talking about, or how to avoid them...nice, D

-0:27:09 Huh...summer renovations has entrance to Gryffindor common room on a different wall! Seems inconvenient

-0:29:10 Wow, the grounds sure seem a lot bigger than previous years. Plus somebody went to the trouble of moving the Whomping Willow! (Bet that was a task!)

-0:31:50 Hagrid's cabin was moved quite a ways too, and they added a room or two at the same time!

-0:34:05 Let's see, keep track of necessary End-Of-Story-Adventure supplies. Harry'll need Hippogriff training—okay, we can check that off...

-0:35:00 Buckbeak effect <u>very</u> well done

-0:35:12 Hagrid clearly said "Let him come to you," yet Harry keeps moving forward—dumb kid

-0:38:46 Ghost comes through Hogwarts window to the sound of breaking glass? He broke some...ghost glass? Whahuh?

-0:39:22 "He's been sighted! Sirius Black!" This is said loud enough for the hall to hear—why does only the Gryffindor table react?

-0:40:55 This isn't really a nit, I suppose...but the Harry Potter books-on-CD and the movie pronounce the word "Ridiculus" differently

-0:44:30 Lucky the giant spider, giant snake, etc. don't <u>attack</u> anybody during the (admittedly) very interesting Boggart lesson

-0:45:28 Now there's a giant pendulum in the Hogwarts entrance—and there are continuity problems with it. It swings right here, shot changes and it swings right again

-0:46:10 Dementors attack a person using their worst memories. How does Harry remember his parents' deaths, seeing as he was a baby when it happened?

-0:48:40 Oh no! The fat lady was attacked! Let's just <u>wonder</u> who did it, rather than asking any of the other 300 paintings within eye- and earshot!

-0:49:50 The main door is now locked and locked and locked again. With what point? Black got in some secret way anyhow

-0:54:10 Quidditch during a thunderstorm? This school has terrible priorities

-0:59:37 Okay, checking off necessary supplies—
Harry has the Marauder's Map, good, that'll be important...

-0:59:00 Harry's trying to sneak to Hogsmead, he's
under the invisibility cloak...and cleverly heads through the
snow <u>right</u> towards Fred and George. Dumb kid

-1:01:00 There's a guy in the cellar as Harry stumps
up the stairs where he shouldn't be—how come nobody says
anything?

-1:01:30 What is the point of Harry swiping Neville's
lollipop? Kinda rude

-1:01:40 So Harry's got a lollipop in his invisibility
cloaked hand. Either his hand should be visible, or the treat
shouldn't—but no sense that the lollipop just looks like it's
levitating, fully visible

-1:02:30 How does one throw a snowball without
some part of one's body leaving the confines of one's
invisibility cloak?

-1:02:33 Throwballs from afar become a close-up
attack—yet no sound of running, and how did he cover the
ground in two seconds? Ninja Potter!

-1:04:10 His cloak being rare, valuable and
irreplaceable, seems like Harry is really cavalier about it

-1:08:09 Is there some Defense Against the Dark Arts
point to the creepy <u>spine</u> candles?

-1:08:30 Continuity as wand comes out of pocket

-1:16:45 Using the Marauder's Map, Harry searches
the hallway for Peter Pettigrew. Okay, so he wouldn't be
expecting a human to be a rat. But can't he even <u>see</u> the rat
scurrying around him?

-1:21:15 Crystal balls come complete with sound
effects? Neat!

-1:22:48 This school has issues. Here the summoned executioner of Buckbeak sits in the school courtyard, calmly sharpening a giant axe. Unacceptable around <u>children</u>!

-1:25:30 Nice of the movers to add all these rooms onto Hagrid's house

-1:26:45 I'm not going to go crazy with the traveling-through-time nits, I swear…but the <u>first</u> time Harry is in Hagrid's house, it's impossible for him to also be outside throwing stones at himself. At the very least that has to happen a <u>second</u> time to happen at all

-1:28:30 Sure is nice of the Whomping Willow to knock Harry and Hermione through the air in slo-motion

-1:32:00 After the Whomping Willow adventure, all that swinging around, there is one, repeat <u>one</u> scratch on Hermione's face???

-1:32:20 Sirius Black and Professor Lupin talk about killing someone. "We've gotta kill him, I'm gonna kill him," and so forth. Throughout, Harry thinks they're talking about him—sure would make a lot of sense and save a lot of trouble for <u>one</u> of these adults to say "Oh, Harry, we're not talking about you," or <u>something</u>!

-1:34:10 "Expelliarmus!" Usually this spell causes a wand to go flying. In previous movies, in later movies…only right here, Snape himself goes for a tumble. Why?

-1:39:47 Pettigrew goes back to being a rat, and leaves his clothes behind. So…why was he wearing clothes when he previously turned into a human? (Not that I'm complaining, mind you…)

-1:40:30 Harry's trying to talk to a werewolf—and his wand is in his <u>pocket</u>? Dumb kid

-1:41:50 Sure is lucky Harry doesn't get shredded by the werewolf, especially since the first time through, he couldn't possibly also be down the hill calling the werewolf away

-1:42:54 By the lake, the spring lake starts turning to ice. Harry watches this happen for <u>twenty seconds</u>, knowing it means Dementors, yet his wand is still in his pocket. Dumb kid

-1:43:45 The Dementor soul-suck very well done...but sure is a lot for a PG rating

-1:45:19 How can Harry see himself on the other side of the lake, when he hasn't <u>yet</u> gone back in time to be on the other side of the lake...

-1:47:34 Okay, so Hermione has the time-turner, Harry has hippogriff riding ability and the marauder's map, they know Pettigrew and Sirius' secrets...think we're ready for the finale!

-1:47:49 Sure is lucky it doesn't hurt to come into contact with yourself while time traveling!

-1:48:00 Watch during the backtiming—there's some poor kid in the hospital wing wrapped in bandages. Never explained

-1:49:00 Yes, I think the fact that a third-year student is granted a dangerous, difficult-to-use, valuable, expensive and likely irreplaceable <u>time-turner</u> for no good reason deserves the Will Award!!!

-1:49:53 "We mustn't be seen." They use the word <u>mustn't</u>, and it seems to be extremely critical. Yet they kinda saunter out in the open, out where their past selves could turn and easily see them

-1:52:30 Harry and Hermione watch themselves plus Ron in the past—but their past selves aren't doing things <u>exactly</u> like they did before! It's all happening faster, for one thing

-1:57:55 Things happening faster here too

-1:58:50 Since the werewolf can run a <u>lot</u> faster than our heroes, sure is lucky he chooses not to, thereby saving their lives

-2:02:28 Knowing that Sirius is going to be taken, why do Harry and Hermione just let it happen?

-2:03:00 Well, at least they can get him out of prison...and as they do so, flying away on Buckbeak, there's all sorts of whooping and carrying-on. This is a <u>prison break</u>, guys! Shhhh!

-2:05:18 Wow these two are in shape! From the courtyard below up five flights of stairs in ten seconds...and they're not even out of breath!

-2:06:00 One would think the birds around here would figure out that the Whomping Willow likes to bat them out of the air...

#29:   Spider-Man 2

<u>Ruminations:</u> I am a self-professed comic geek (I'm not that great with math, I can't fix computers...a guy's gotta have <u>something,</u>) and putting aside the interior webbing issue mentioned on the previous review, Marvel is doing a bang-up job with the Spider-man movies. One of the things they really get right is how Peter just can't catch a break. I really noticed

that in this movie, as did my own mother. I saw Spidey 2 for the first time with my folks--at the planetarium party, when Peter goes to reach for a canapé and the last one disappears out from under his fingers, right then mom leaned over in the theater and whispered, "Does he <u>ever</u> get a break?" Sorry, ma...Peter Parker is the original hard-luck Charlie!

    -First shot of the movie--as Parker skids his scooter to a stop, he changes positions between shots. He also changes positions later as his scooter bumps into the carpet van.

    -So Peter's in trouble because he's late for work--and Joe is not going to get his money for the pizzas Parker needs to deliver. Why, then, does Joe waste time telling Parker about the "29-minute guarantee"? Send him on his way, already!

    -Man, those New York drivers. The light goes red on Peter and his scooter, and <u>less than a second</u> later a bus is going through in front of him. At full speed. That's dangerous, man! (Ironically, the bus has a Mary Jane advertisement on it, which I've never noticed before)

    -Is it reasonable to expect <u>eight</u> deep-dish pizzas delivered 42 blocks away in less than 29 minutes? Maybe Joe is the one with the problem...

    -Again with the New York drivers: the truck driver almost hits two kids, and even though Spidey gets them out of the way, the truck driver doesn't even <u>stop</u>?

    -So Pete's got <u>eight</u> pizzas to deliver. He leaves Joe's with eight pizzas, and he puts eight pizzas on the counter by the snooty receptionist. <u>But</u>, when he picks up the pizzas he left on the balcony while rescuing the kids...there's only <u>seven</u> sitting there!

-Pete comes out of the broom closet in his street clothes...yet earlier as he swung away with the pizzas in his Spidey suit, he wasn't carrying any extra bundles. The closet is also in full view of the receptionist; how did Spidey get in there without her seeing him? A broom closet with a skylight?

-It often amazes me how selectively deaf people can be. Mary Jane's in the kitchen with Aunt May, no more than five, six feet from Harry and Peter--but Harry talks about M.J.'s true feelings for Parker in a normal tone of voice, as if she couldn't possibly overhear.

-Of course a subway train goes by <u>right</u> as we see Peter walking in the door of his horrible apartment. (I'm reminded of the apartment in Blues Brothers.)

-Right after we are introduced to Peter's horrible apartment we see a sweeping shot of New York City...and there's a lens flare at the bottom of the shot. I'm calling this one a nit, though the Director of Photography probably saw it--because for my money, if you remind people that they're watching a movie without a really good reason...that's a mistake.

-Harry Osborn switches positions between shots as he walks down Otto's stairs.

-Pete pulls the old "wash something colored with the whites" trick that we all do at least once in our lives, and his Spidey duds turn all his whites pink. He's been living on his own for more than a year, and this is the <u>first</u> time he's done this? (Or is he really that out of it?)

-It's truly incredible, and--yes--perhaps a bit <u>unbelievable</u> that Spidey could in one split-second catch a falling police car, and anchor that car from two different buildings. Also amazing is the <u>strength</u> of those webs to accomplish something like that.

-As the bank robbers try and get away, one of them shoots at the front of the police car, which spins almost 180 degrees to the right...and then in the next shot is pointed straight and spins again.

-The passenger-side bank robber can't make up his mind. In one shot he's firing a submachine gun, then one frame later it's turned into a shotgun.

-Spidey is on the back of the bank robbers' car, they point their guns at him, he webs each gun, then jumps up...and instead of the guns being ripped out of the bank robbers' hands, <u>they</u> get pulled up too. Umm...

-Sometimes Pete gives up way too quickly. Okay, he's late for M.J.'s show, the jerk at the front doors won't let him in...he could still wait for intermission, right? Plus, if Mary Jane's deadbeat <u>dad</u> could get backstage to borrow cash, I refuse to believe <u>Spider-man</u> can't find a way into the theater. He just doesn't know what he wants, that's his problem...

-Pete, on the dead phone: "I'm Spider-man. Now you know why we can't be together. If my enemies found out about you..." <u>What</u> enemies? Has Peter been having adventures and not telling us? Dr. Octopus hasn't been created yet, and the Green Goblin certainly isn't going to be hurting anyone anymore...

-I've never been to New York. Do companies really put up hundreds of the same poster along a building? What purpose does that serve? (Not that I really mind looking at hundreds of images of Kirsten Dunst, but still...)

-Why does Spidey lose and regain his powers? They did this to us in the comics, too, and it didn't make sense then. Does it really happen that a person can be so emotionally confused that they lose physical abilities? (Gee, I had a sense of hearing yesterday...)

-Watching Dr. Octavius begin his experiment, I'm struck by how casual it all is. Sure, he thinks he's figured everything out and it's absolutely safe, but he's performing a never-before-tried experimental procedure using volatile, unstable elements! And there's twenty, thirty people just standing there watching him a few feet away? Tsk tsk, doctor! Maybe if he had taken some <u>precautions</u>, there wouldn't have been so darned much glass available to be thrown around, and his wife wouldn't have been killed...

-Dr. Octavius stands on his pedestal, the spinal bit of the arms aligns with his neck, and the metal needles just <u>push themselves</u> right on into his spinal cord. Does that bother anybody else?

-Where is the camera located in each arm? We see one of the arms snap open from its closed position, yet behind Otto all four arm-camera-shots are visible on the monitor, and none of them change.

-It's a valiant effort, and a very well-designed effect, but Otto's arm-cameras don't quite match up with the views seen on the monitor behind him.

-Forget the cameras, what about the arms themselves? Either they're about six feet long or they're thirty feet long, but they can't be <u>both</u>.

-For whatever reason, Otto's runaway fusion reaction attracts metal, thus making the metal doors at the end of the room buckle and leap towards the experiment. Why, though, does the <u>glass</u> in the doors come with? Sure, it would break, but then gravity should take over...

-It seems unnecessarily theatrical to me that as Otto lies in the operating room, the evil metal arms are draped out around him rather than coiled up out of the way somehow. I dunno, maybe I'm being picky.

-How exactly do the arms react in self-defense when Otto isn't even conscious? Yes, there was a line about "incredibly self-aware" or some such, but <u>come on...</u>

-Each arm has a camera "eye" right in the center. Yet one of these same arms can extend a foot-long spike right from its center too. Where does the camera go when this happens--and why would any of these created-to-aid-science arms need a long <u>spike?</u>

-Otto stumbles out of the hospital, grabs a taxicab and throws it away from himself, and it's almost about to hit the empty street...when the shot changes and suddenly it lands on another cab. Huh?

-It's ever-so-slightly farfetched that a half-naked guy in a hospital gown, being propelled by four mechanical arms, could go into hiding--even in New York.

-At least some New Yorkers are thoughtful--like whoever abandoned the half-demolished building on the pier. They left the lights on when they went, just in case some supervillain needed a place to stay.

-And then because the arms can think for themselves, it makes perfect sense that they can...somehow...mentally communicate with their host. (Sure doesn't take much persuasion for the good Doctor to go over to the dark side, either)

-The cops rush over to Dr. Octopus, who just ripped the door of the bank vault off its hinges and threw it away...but they still give him a chance to surrender. (Shoot him from a distance, somebod--well, maybe the cops outside the bank will shoo--oh, never mind, it's too late)

-As Doc Ock prepares to skewer Spidey, Aunt May clocks him with her umbrella...and Doc's head changes positions between shots during the slow-motion montage.

-Spidey drops to the ground with Aunt May, says "There you go," and in the _instant_ the shot changes from a wide to a close-up, an extra 30 or so people suddenly appear in-frame behind them.

-We all noticed Spider-man creator Stan Lee save the woman in the street, right? Just checking.

-I don't know if this is a nit or not--maybe it's just me--but it feels like 7/8ths of the New Yorkers we get a good, long look at are all attractive twenty-something females. (That Big Apple is one swingin' town, I tell ya...)

-The cops apparently aren't much, though: they have _eight full seconds_ to shoot at Doc Ock while he casually strolls around the corner of the building, and they don't hit anything vital.

-_The Will Award_: lucky for Aunt May (and Peter) that Spider-man's powers failed him only _once_ during the whole bank-robbery-chase-Doc-Ock-up-the-building event. Sure would have been a shame if his webbing vanished during those moments he had to save Aunt May from falling to her death...

-I don't get out to high-society events much, but based on what I know from the movies, there must be one person at every function whose sole responsibility is to watch for emotional, important moments and signal to the band to _immediately_ stop playing. (He's working overtime at the planetarium party.)

-We were talking about lost spider abilities...how it is possible for Petey to _lose_ his spider-clinging ability? After all, he now has those nifty _spines_ that come right out of his _fingers_... (grumble mumble grumble)

-Not that you necessarily care, but when Peter says in his dream to Uncle Ben "I'm Spider-man no more," that references the title of Amazing Spider-Man #50, where Parker tried to give up being a superhero. The shot of him walking away from his Spidey suit in the trash can references the cover of that same comic. (Did I mention being a comic geek?)

-Lens flare on the camera as Peter walks away from his newly thrown-away Spider suit. (The costume designers must have <u>loved</u> that shot, especially since each suit cost around $100,000 <u>each</u>.)

-More lens flare at the beginning of the "Raindrops keep falling on my head" montage. By now I'm <u>certain</u> the filmmakers are aware of all this, but it bugs me, so it's a nit. (Phhhhhhbt!)

-In the "Raindrops falling on my head" montage, where Peter ain't gonna play at Spidey no more, he buys a hot-dog, turns around and calmly watches several police vehicles go by, sirens blazing. At the same time several uniformed cops are running down the street towards him. It looks like the two are related, but...do the cops on foot have any hope of arriving to whatever's going on before it's over? (Gasp, heave, "Put your-" pant, gasp, "hands up-" gasp, "punk!"

-Early in that same montage, Peter falls out of frame as he's walking, the shot changes...and he's in a completely different location as he gets back up.

-We see Peter go to the doctor, and I can't help but wonder what the doc thinks when he takes a look at Peter's highly unusual, radioactive isotope-charged blood sample.

-Where does Dr. Octopus <u>get</u> the materials he uses to build his giant second-try fusion reactor? Local supervillain-friendly Home Depot? Then after he builds his special toy, he clomps his way through New York to Harry Osborn's house-- despite being a wanted fugitive--and no police in sight.

-Spider-man really had been busy. He quits, and within days crime is up "75%". What about the X-Men, Daredevil, the Avengers, the Fantastic Four, and--oh yeah-- the police? (It's also interesting how the Daily Bugle, which had labeled Spidey a menace, is so quick to turn on itself and ask "Where's Spider-man now?" with the new crime-wave.

-Like the last movie, the back-and-forth outdoor conversations between Peter and Mary Jane have continuity issues. After Peter finally sees M.J.'s play, as they stand on the sidewalk, the shot changes right before Mary Jane says "I'm getting married." There's a woman who passes out of frame to the right and should pop behind Mary Jane as the shot cuts to her...but she never does.

-We hear the woman screaming "Fuego!" (i.e., "Fire!") but don't hear the fire until the camera turns to show us. (I, personally, can hear things behind me that I'm not looking at. Peter apparently does not have the same ability. Maybe that's something he lost when the spider DNA replaced his own?)

-So during the scene in the burning building...um...the little three-year-old kid helps pull Peter up out of the hole in the floor? Whaaaah?

-Can anybody explain to me the point of the "Would you like a piece of chocolate cake" scene, with Peter's cute young Russian neighbor? (They might as well have put up an INTERMISSION sign and been done with it!)

-Peter shows up at Aunt May's for moving day. Aunt May is packing a box (towel in hand,) and the shot changes right before she says "Pish tosh"--and her position changes when the shot does. This happens again as she's putting shoes in a box and Peter's talking to Henry.

-When Peter runs across the rooftop in his street clothes, determined to get his powers back, there's something red reflected in his glasses...but nothing red on the rooftop.

-Dr. Octopus is on his way to find Peter. Who told him Pete would be at the café, and how does he get there without attracting attention? (Take the bus?) Up to the moment where the car comes through the café window, people on the street are just about their normal business. Nobody's pointing, or running, or shouting... Also, Doc finds Peter in order to find Spider-man. So Doc Ock kinda needs to get some information from Peter. Does it make <u>any</u> sense to announce himself by throwing a car through the café window? If not for Peter's incredible reflexes, he and Mary Jane would have been killed.

-So Doc Ock throws a car through the café window (just saying hello in his own special way) and one of the car's tires <u>just</u> misses Pete's head, and Pete is on the floor, so the car must be more-or-less upright. The very next frame shows a wider shot of the car...and the <u>roof</u> is pointing at the ground while the <u>wheels</u> are up.

-Peter's Spider-sense is truly amazing. It not only warns him that there's danger behind him, but is so specific about <u>what</u> danger that he knows there's a car coming through the window and he needs to grab M.J. and leap forward out of the way. He never looks behind him, just reacts. What a gift!

-Ock takes M.J., Peter runs out of the café and suddenly realizes he doesn't need his glasses anymore. He takes them off, puts them back on...and for some reason his <u>hearing</u> (the movie sound) dims when he puts his glasses back on! I wear glasses myself, I'm sure glad I don't go deaf when I'm not wearing them.

-Sure wish they'd shown us Peter grabbing his costume back from Jameson's office--considering that he got in, grabbed his costume, webbed up the thank-you note and got out in under <u>two seconds</u>...that must have been some stunt!

-How lucky that as Ock and Spidey fight each other they fall <u>onto</u> the El train, rather than in front of it...

-When Dr. Octopus breaks the controls in the El train, we see the speed gauge, which runs from 0 to 120. <u>A hundred and twenty</u>? On an El train?

-And since <u>when</u> are there Els in New York anyway?

-As Spidey realizes the train's brakes are gone, he takes a long look at the track in front of him--and apparently suddenly borrows Superman's telescopic vision, because he seems to realize that two miles down the road the track comes to an end.

-After Spider-man saves the train, and Peter starts to fall, hands reach out to catch him and the sound guy forgot to include the sound effect as they open the train door--because it's closed when he starts to fall, open when they get him back, but no sound between.

-Doc comes onto the train to collect Spider-man and knocks him unconscious. As Spidey falls, he changes position between shots.

-Peter must have stopped on the way to Doc Ock's hideout to clean his mask--because it's all better when he arrives.

-All of the things Doc Ock does to Spidey as they fight...he seems to be forgetting he's supposed to bring Spider-man to Harry Osborn--<u>alive</u>--before he'll get his tritium. (Perhaps he doesn't care anymore. Gee, this guy used to be kinda nice. Shame what happened. That's what you get for performing dangerous experiments without proper precautions...)

-I've been mean enough, time for something good: the sequence where Peter saves the train is <u>incredible</u>, one of the best action-film moments I've ever seen. I find myself straining along with him, trying to help him stop the train. Then when the passengers step in front of Peter to keep him from Doc Ock, it brings tears to my eyes every time. Kudos!

-Spider-man tore his mask off while on top of the train...I can't imagine how it managed to get <u>inside</u> for the kids to hand it back to him later.

-Lucky nobody took a cell-phone pic of Parker while his mask was off

-Doctor Octopus makes off with Spider-man, is next seen climbing back to Harry Osborn's penthouse...and he <u>still</u> keeps eluding the police! (They're just not trying!)

-Does it make sense for Harry Osborn to keep the radioactive, <u>incredibly</u> rare and expensive tritium (a large gob of it, in fact) in the safe at his <u>house</u>? Don't they have secure laboratories for this kind of thing?

-Harry tells Peter where to find Mary Jane. How does Harry know where Dr. Octopus is going to be? "Hey, Harry, if you need me, I'll be--you know that old, crappy building down off of third? Yeah, that one. I'll be there executing my evil scheme if anybody calls."

-I'll bet the EPA is really excited about this huge fusion reaction being dumped into the Hudson river.

-Peter grabs Mary Jane and swings away from Doc's final resting place...<u>what</u> is he swinging on? The whole building has gone down into the river! And how <u>deep</u> is the Hudson, anyway? Doc just sinks and sinks and sinks into the dark...

-Spider-man lowers Mary Jane from the crane on a strand of webbing. She's well below the level of the crane, the shot changes to the arriving police car with her fiancée, back to her...and she drops past the crane again. Is Spidey using M.J. as a yo-yo?

-So Harry Osborn takes up the Green Goblin mantle. Is madness hereditary? Or does Norman's ghost conveniently show up to spur his son on? (Both explanations seem a little flimsy, as does the premise that this big, Green Goblin storeroom has been just waiting around to be discovered for the past two years...)

-When Harry goes loopy and throws the knife through the mirror, he changes positions between the closeup where he screams "No!" and the shot where he throws the knife. (And as long as you're freeze-framing <u>that</u>, watch the next shot of the mirror. One frame is Norman, one is Harry yelling at himself, then the mirror breaks on an image of Norman...a nice touch you can't even see in real-time!)

-As Harry steps through the (broken) looking glass, the first five, six steps he takes should be accompanied by broken glass sounds--but they're not.

-Peter, Mr. Spider-sense, must be <u>really</u> zoned out, as I refuse to believe Mary Jane got all the way up the stairs to his apartment, in her wedding dress, without making a sound.

-This happens a <u>lot</u> in movies: Peter and Mary Jane come together for their first kiss (finally!), and as Peter moves in his head is tilted to the left. Shot changes, and his head is tilted to the right.

-Neither Peter nor Mary Jane think much of the NYPD...they're sharing their first kiss, a siren goes by, and immediately they both think Spider-man needs to leave. Can't the cops handle things just <u>once</u>? Furthermore, Peter smiles, turns, M.J. runs to the window and Spider-man swings away. As well as borrowing Superman's telescopic vision, Spidey must have also cribbed his super speed...because I don't know how else he got into costume <u>that</u> fast.

-I would imagine that New York police helicopter pilots positively <u>hate</u> Spider-man. The webslinger better be more careful around choppers, that would be a really stupid way to die...

#30:   Indiana Jones and the Raiders of the Lost Ark

<u>Ruminations:</u> If you didn't read the Foreword to this book (and why not, may I ask? I'm not writing just to hear myself talk) you might be surprised to see <u>Raiders</u> here instead of <u>Crystal Skull</u>. Go back and read it, and you'll not be surprised anymore.

I chose this movie out of the original trilogy because it introduces the character and in my mind is still the best.

Loved Crusade, don't get me wrong, and Temple of Doom has its moments, but Raiders is the best. And I wondered if I would find many nits to pick. Boy, did I! The truck chase alone could fill a book!

It's also interesting that the filmmakers chose a real, historical article as the item Indy goes after, rather than making something up like they did in Temple of Doom or Last Crusade. There may be a lot of mythology surrounding the Ark of the Covenant--but it's real, arguably unlike Shankara stones or the Holy Grail. It actually exists, and there are historical documents (i.e., The Bible) describing it. Which helps a Biblically well-read nitpicker, let me tell you!

One last note: if you've been around movies for long, you may have heard that Tom Selleck was chosen to be Indiana Jones originally, but couldn't get out of Magnum P.I. Well, you may not know--Indiana Jones also coulda been Steve Martin, Bill Murray, or Chevy Chase! Matter of fact, Harrison Ford was picked only three weeks out from the first day of shooting! (The More You Know...)

...seriously, Steve Martin as Indiana Jones?

-0:00:54 Not really a nit, but Alfred Moline (see Dr. Octopus in previous review) sure has come a long way from being a throwaway Indiana Jones lackey!

-0:02:26 "Movitos are here. They're following us." Evidence of this is a dart already in the tree. How is the dart already there, if the Movitos are following our hero?

-0:03:13 Indy has a loaded, cocked gun pointed at his back. Lucky the guy who is completely ready to shoot him doesn't do so during the coupla seconds Indy's getting his whip on

-0:03:20 Why did the guy draw down on Indy anyway?

-0:04:05 Jones grabs a bag of sand outside the temple—did he <u>know</u> he would need it later? Or does he just go around with bags of sand a lot?

-0:04:50 There are no spiders on the cobwebs Indy and Satipo step through—yet suddenly at this point they're covered with tarantulas. From where?

And by the way eeeeeeeuuuuuuggggghhhhh!!!!! I don't mind a roomful of snakes later, but all these big 'ol spiders here...

-0:05:33 Indy waves a hand through the light, and blocking said light trips a booby trap. So...this trap only works at certain times of day?

-0:06:50 Freeze frame as the dart supposedly hits the club Indy's holding—looks like the dart actually springs out of the club haft. Which would be weird, in real-life grave-robbing...er, archaeology

-0:07:25 There's a light on the little golden statue, and I'm flummoxed as to where it is coming from

-0:07:39 Even if this little cute statue is hollow, if that's gold, no way a coupla pounds of sand equals the weight, even before Indy takes some sand <u>out</u>

-0:08:06 Indy pulls famous switcheroo, and thinks he's gotten away with it. Why does it take the stone six seconds to decide to drop? Drama-equipped booby trap?

-0:08:18 Amazing that <u>none</u> of the poison darts connect as Indy races away

-0:08:44 Lucky that there's <u>just</u> enough time to get through that closing door

-0:08:58 Indy's hanging by his elbows, scrabbling at a root that keeps getting longer. He's hanging by his elbows, and he's a tough guy—why can't he lever himself up?

-0:09:13 Obvious dummy, not Satipo in booby trap

-0:09:22 This one makes me laugh. As a farewell, Indy turns and says goodbye to, and I quote, "Sapito." Except the guy's name (check the credits!) is <u>Satipo</u>

-0:09:25 Perfectly round...ginormous...<u>boulder</u>? Just sitting around waiting to roll down on somebody?

-0:11:27 Angry Movitos chasing Indy, and about 10 yards behind him. Shot changes, and now they're 100 yards back! They all get winded?

-0:12:00 Lucky no arrows or spears hit Indy during his daring escape

-0:12:10 Two-seater plane. Did Indy plan to ditch Satipo and friends, or did he somehow know they wouldn't be coming?

-0:16:12 Fibbies talking to Indy and Brody. "This is strictly confidential." Which is why they're talking about it in this open, echoey, unlocked hall!

-0:17:23 Indy says the ark contains the tablets Moses brought down from Mount Sinai and smashed, "If you believe in that sort of thing." The ark really existed, as I talked about previously, and inside were (are!) <u>not</u> the smashed tablets, but rather the second version which Moses was forced to go back up Mount Sinai to get. Along with some manna, and Aaron's rod which budded in front of the Egyptians. And for the record, Indy—I <u>do</u> believe in that sort of thing!

-0:18:10 So the city where the Ark supposedly disappeared to endured a <u>year-long</u> sandstorm? Has any sandstorm in history lasted anywhere <u>near</u> 12 months?

-0:19:18 Indy says he's "not an expert" on the Staff of Ra...for not an expert, he sure knows a lot about it!

-0:19:42 Indy flips open a giant book—Bible?—and it stops <u>right</u> at a picture of the Ark

-0:20:00 They talk about lightning coming from the Ark. No lightning comes out of the Ark at any point in

Scripture. Uzzah is struck down by God when he reaches out to touch the Ark (2 Samuel 6:7) but no lightning

-0:20:14 "The Bible speaks of the Ark leveling mountains, and laying waste to entire regions." Um, no, it doesn't. This is annoying because this movie makes the Ark out to be almost sinister, but it was a treasure of the Israelites. Yes, being connected to God, this treasure needed to be properly treated—but it wasn't an instrument of evil

-0:20:23 The whole premise of the movie is that if the Nazis get the Ark, they'll be super powerful. I don't think God would support the Nazis even if they had the Ark (didn't work for the Philistines, after all)

-0:22:38 Indy on the plane—continuity issue as shot changes

-0:23:24 Ah, the often copied Red-Line Travel Service. Not a nit, just a note: on the long trip to Nepal, Indy had a stopover in Hawaii and another in Japan

-0:25:24 Open bar door has a light coming in from outside. Nepalese streetlamp, perhaps?

-0:26:30 Folks have been searching for the Ark for 3,000 years—awful convenient that the necessary puzzle piece just happens to be readily available

-0:27:38 Light is awfully steady if it's firelight—and unexplained if not

-0:28:11 And of course Marion just happens to have the Ra eye thingy around her neck

-0:28:49 Is Marion knew to this bar-running business? She leaves $3,000 in cash winnings just sitting in a cigar box on the bar? Somehow I don't think this is a very safe neighborhood

-0:30:32 Weird light on Toht's face here

-0:30:38 continuity—Marion's face was forward, shot changes and it's sideways

-0:38:46 continuity again—Marion face side to front

-0:31:00 Sure is lucky Indy decided to come back, huh?

-0:32:39 Toht's hand is burning—he holds on for four whole seconds? This is some tough guy

-0:33:50 More Red Line Travel—stopovers in Karachi and Baghdad on the way to Cairo

-0:36:18 Of the Ark: "Death has always surrounded it. It is not of this earth." Do I have to repeat myself at this point? People <u>have</u> died because of the Ark—but it has <u>not</u> always been surrounded by death! And an Israelite craftsman made it, (Bezalel, if you're curious—Exodus 37) the Ark itself is not supernatural

-0:38:40 Continuity—Indy hits bad guy, shot change, he hits him again

-0:39:30 You can lose a hand, stealing something in the Middle East. Yet somehow Marion gets away with a whole frying pan? (Sure, she uses it for good purpose, but theft is theft)

-0:40:24 Famous shot where Indy is facing Dude-With-Sword and he just shoots him. According to what I hear, Harrison Ford was suffering from dysentery on the day they were <u>supposed</u> to shoot a big fight scene, and this was the agreed-upon compromise (The More You Know...)

-0:41:17 Continuity as Indy breaks out of crowd

-0:41:30 Sure is lucky Indy isn't hit, with that guy machine-gunning everything

-0:45:20 "The Ark is a transmitter. It's a radio for speaking to God." Long suffering sigh...no it's not! They had a whole Temple for that...

-0:45:45 Sallah sends his children in to rescue Indy from the bad guys—nice of Sallah to consider Indiana over the lives of his own children!

-0:49:19 So, the previously intelligent monkey didn't realize the dates were poisoned! Nice of him to take one for the team, eh? And sure is lucky Sallah noticed and made the connection in time!

-0:51:28 Sure is lucky the all-important Map Room wasn't harmed during the <u>year-long</u> sandstorm, huh?

-0:54:00 wow, that beam of light sure is <u>loud</u>

-0:54:55 Indy's extremely not-Arabic face is in full view—lucky no Nazi notices

-0:55:09 Marion's not dead after all! Sure is lucky Indy stumbles across her, huh?

-0:56:15 Yeah, I'm sure the Nazis would have no time to investigate the American...with the sextant...standing on the ridge in plain view

-0:57:30 So Toht just managed to get a <u>legible</u> burn of the doohickey?

-0:58:30 Yeah, I'm sure the Nazis would pay <u>no</u> attention to the group digging out-of-bounds, even the one with the leather jacket and fedora (he sure must be sweaty, huh? Leather jacket in the desert heat?)

-1:00:00 When they pry the lid off this burial chamber, air rushes out as though it's been airtight all this time. So...what have all those snakes been breathing for the past 1,000 years? What did they eat?

-1:00:35 Since when do many different kinds of snakes hang out? There are boas and asps and cobras in here...

-1:02:30 I'm sure I don't know, but that doesn't look like a 1936 bra Marion takes off

-1:02:40 And the dress just <u>happens</u> to fit Marion

-1:02:44 Arm continuity on Marion as shot changes

-1:02:50 Continuity as Marion turns

-1:03:10 Continuity as Indy goes down the rope. He pushes off from the statue, then next frame he's flipped 180 degrees

-1:03:34 I think they fixed this one for the DVD release, but get an old enough VHS copy and you can see the firelight reflected in the glass between Harrison Ford and the deadly cobra

-1:04:08 ...and the convenient gas can with pump came from where?

-1:05:32 sure is bright in this torchlit room

-1:06:42 Continuity—this happens often in movies. Watch the wine level in the bottle, it jumps up and down as the shot changes

-1:08:10 nice touch with Toht and his collapsible coat hanger—as a trained ninja, I can attest that would still make a <u>great</u> weapon!

-1:08:37 Sure is lucky the poles were there for the carrying, and that two people can do the work reserved historically for 6. And oh...by the way...though the length/height/width of the ark, and the cherubim on top, seem pretty accurate, the filmmakers missed or deliberately changed one detail. Exodus 37 has a detailed description of the Ark of the Covenant, including the fact that the rings the poles go through for carrying were attached to the <u>feet</u> of the Ark, not the <u>top</u>!

As someone who is very fond of Biblical history, and the Ark, I'm tempted to give this the Will Award, but I'm gonna hang on to that one for awhile...

-1:08:50 No Biblical reason why the ark should shine like that

-1:09:40 ...and the rope to raise the Ark came from where?

-1:10:40 Continuity, Belloq's position on the chamber rim

-1:10:50 Continuity—from one frame to the next, Belloq shifts about a foot to his left

-1:11:27 Looking up at Marion as she dangles from the statue...are those black running shorts under her dress?

-1:11:36 Continuity—Marion falls, and just as she almost hits the floor the shot changes and she's suddenly in Indy's arms

-1:13:46 As Indy climbs the statue he sees...is that a rattlesnake? (They've got all kinds of snakes in here!!)

-1:14:45 Another peek up Marion's dress—and she took the shorts off at some point

-1:14:53 Before Indy and Marion broke into this room, there were snakes oozing through the holes. Once in...all snakes gone?

-1:14:59 Marion uncovers dead guy—and somebody other than her starts screaming. Where is this coming from?

-1:15:15 Now there's a whole chorus of screams. Is the Nazi Glee Club back here somewhere?

-1:15:20 Maybe this is supposed to represent Marion's fears more than reality? She's 3-deep in skeletons, then suddenly Indy is there and most of the bodies disappear. Were they in her mind?

-1:15:33 Sure is lucky they found a way out, huh?

-1:15:35 Continuity—as the shot changes, Indy goes from backing out of the window to suddenly leaning in

-1:15:40 Huh. Same with Marion! These two really are alike!

-1:16:00 Lucky nobody sees Indy peeking waaaaay over that barrel

-1:16:30 Is there really a trunk in this flying wing that the Ark will fit into?

-1:17:27 Continuity—a closeup shot of Marion pulling chocks from the wheel, then cut to a wide shot which shows all three wheels—and no Marion

-1:17:58 Continuity in the fight scene (no, I'm not going to tell you what. You go look)

-1:18:53 Since the bullets are hitting the <u>ground</u>, why does the Nazi fall? He get hit in the toe?

-1:19:10 Big explosion, and suddenly all Nazis are on alert. What have they been doing during the last thirty seconds, while all the gunfire was going on?

-1:19:18 Why is <u>Belloq</u> the grave-robber going to check out the scene?

-1:20:20 Propeller Nazi-bits...pretty graphic for PG movie

-1:27:15 "I dunno, I'm making this up as I go." Whether that was in the script or an ad-lib on the day I am uncertain—but one of the best lines <u>ever</u>!! I know I'm nitpicking pretty hard, but I still love this movie!!!

-1:23:00 Convenient that Indy didn't get lost or delayed as he went cross-country on horseback

-1:24:16 Indy punches the truck driver as trees flash past the passenger window. Next frame the trees are gone and the driver falls out and off a cliff. Next shot the trees are back! (The close-ups for most of this scene were filmed on a tree-lined road, and the wide shots were not—makes editing kinda difficult, though I never noticed til I started looking)

-1:24:34 More tree continuity

-1:24:48 Continuity again—this time it's wet windshield/dry windshield/wet windshield

-1:25:34 Continuity—wide shot has jeep diving off a magically appearing cliff, on a mountain road. Shot changes and mountain road and cliff are gone

-1:26:29 Continuity—stuntman hanging on the door

-1:26:41 Appearing/disappearing cliff

-1:27:01 More tree continuity

-1:27:16 Stuntman flipping over truck continuity

-1:27:29 Indy sure is amazing—holding on to the truck with his wounded shoulder and everything!

-1:27;40 Lucky nobody in that Nazi-filled car up front shoots Indy while he wrestles on the front of the truck, huh?

-1:27:56 Also lucky they don't <u>stop</u> the truck and get him off there

-1:28:08 No nit--but just take a moment to be amazed at what that dragged-behind-the-moving-truck stuntman had to endure!

-1:28:50 Indy's back in control of the truck, and still nobody in the Nazi car shoots him

-1:29:25 Careening into town, Indy drives right into a stall, they lower the curtain and the Nazis can't find him. He's "making this up as he goes"...how'd he set that up from the road? By cell-phone?

-1:29:50 It's just the one courtyard, the Nazis know Indy's around here somewhere—lucky they don't start searching and shooting folks

-1:29:57 How long since the rescue, and Marion still has that tattered dress on? Are there no clothes in this country?

-1:31:12 What a tough guy—Indy reaches out with his bullet-wounded arm for Marion, and doesn't even wince

-1:31:39 Grungy, but here on the wide shot of the steamship, obviously had to be taken from another ship probably at great expense—there's a smudge on the lens

-1:32:04 Quick change artist! Indy had his jacket on two seconds ago—now he's out of it, and silently! Indiana Ninja!

-1:32:31 Continuity—the bandage on Indy's arm gets about 2x bigger

-1:35:08 Bandage back to normal

-1:38:05 Have I mentioned how lucky Indy is? We see him on the Nazi sub, he waves at the steamship and then kinda looks around, concerned. If I were him I'd be concerned too—as soon as they dive, he's a drowned grave-robber...er, archaeologist.

Here's the thing. For some unexplained, unlikely reason, the sub <u>never completely submerges</u>. They don't show how Indy hangs on, though the movie novelization I owned as a kid mentioned him lashing himself to the periscope. Regardless...what are the odds that the Nazis would choose for no good reason to leave their sub <u>just</u> out of the water, all the way to their <u>hidden, secret Nazi base</u>?

That's right, ladies and gentlemen...this one earns the Will Award for outstanding cinematic ridiculousness!

-1:38:58 Indy drags pudgy Nazi over some boxes—nice of the chap not to cry out as he is assaulted, no?

-1:39:33 The coat is too <u>tight</u> for Indy? The guy was kinda chubby, shouldn't it be the other way around? (And who was this Nazi related to, that he could get away with his physical condition around a "genetically superior" bunch of goose-steppers?)

-1:41:02 Lucky that the Nazi military discipline is so sloppy that Indy can just sneak around in plain view

-1:41:20 Poor Karen Allen—half the movie in a flimsy dress, now she's in a flimsy nightie. Traveling the terrain in those shoes can't be a picnic either

-1:42:22 Observation and kudos: Paul Freeman, playing Belloq, finishes his scene here, despite the fact that a fly has landed on his lip and crawled <u>into his mouth</u>!

And have you ever noticed that before? This nitpicking can be fun, no?

-1:44:00 Sure is lucky they don't <u>just kill Indy</u> when he surrenders, huh?

-1:44:28 I've been giving the filmmakers a hard time about the Ark—here's a kudos: near as I can tell, the ephod that Belloq wears as he opens the Ark is accurate to scriptural description

-1:44:46 Two of the Nazis <u>touch</u> the Ark? <u>Here</u> is where people oughta be struck dead—but nothing happens

-1:45:06 And whose idea was it that the Ark be filled with <u>sand</u>?

-1:46:00 And whose idea was it that <u>ghosts</u> come out of the Ark? Read 1 Samuel 6:19 for a description of what happens when the ark is opened—no ghosts or evil spirits or avenging angels are mentioned

-1:46:33 Why are Indy and Marion tied to a giant eyeball on a stick?

-1:47:23 While not scripturally accurate, the lightning-through-the-Nazis effect is very well done (back when they didn't have computers to do everything either, no less)

-1:47:38 The melting faces are well done too, but how in the world did this movie get a PG rating? And whose idea was it for melting faces...never mind

-1:47:46 None of the Ark opening scene really makes sense, so I guess it shouldn't make sense that not-looking saves Indy and Marion's lives

-1:48:50 The lid of the Ark comes back down out of the heavens, and all is quiet save for a...cricket chirping? How did said cricket escape the demonic lightning devastation that just ran roughshod across this little island?

-1:49:00 Okay, so all the Nazis are lightning-ed or melted or whatever, leaving Marion and Indy alone on the island. All the equipment is blown. Even granting that the crew left on the submarine somehow escaped the Ark Devastation...how exactly do Indy and Marion get back home? Commandeer the sub? Swim?

Maybe the Ark magically sent them home...

Afterword

Thanks for playing--and keep up looking for nits! If you just couldn't get enough, www.slipups.com has more, as well as Volumes 4 & 5 of this very series...

But I gotta go back to the movies...

38754889R00089

Printed in Poland
by Amazon Fulfillment
Poland Sp. z o.o., Wrocław